Thread
of Life

an Adoption Story

Mike Doiron

iUniverse

Thread of Life
An Adoption Story

iUniverse books may be ordered through booksellers or by contacting:

iUniverse
1663 Liberty Drive
Bloomington, IN 47403
www.iuniverse.com
1-800-Authors (1-800-288-4677)

ISBN: 978-1-4759-8215-2 (sc)
ISBN: 978-1-4759-8217-6 (hc)
ISBN: 978-1-4759-8216-9 (e)

Library of Congress Control Number: 2013905085

Print information available on the last page.

iUniverse rev. date: 03/14/2017

"Gaining access to that interior life is a kind of ... Archeology: on the basis of some information and a little bit of guesswork you journey to a site to see what remains were left behind and you reconstruct the world"

— Toni Morrison

Ever hear the expression 'what you don't know would fill a book'?
Well here it is.

This book documents the true story of a journey that was originally intended to find out some unknowns that perhaps any adopted child may have about their biological history. The intent was to try to fill in some gaps genealogically, medically, and perhaps even mentally as I started out as an adult following university. The journey brought me down a path of self discovery and adventure, that I later started to document for my daughter. After putting to paper my 'adventure findings', I then decided to more formally document and share with others. This is by no means meant as an instruction manual or professional guide to families of adoption, but rather a documented true story sharing personal insights of an adopted journey.

This book is dedicated primarily to adopted children seeking to connect to that 'thread of life', but also to mothers and fathers, especially those who openly invite a child to be part of their family as if conceived by them.

'The chosen One
Not of my Flesh
Nor of my Bone
But still miraculously my own
Never forget a single minute
You didn't grow under my heart, but in it.'

— Anonymous

CONTENTS

1. Meet the Big Apple 1

2. A Boys Roots. 13

3. Harter and Ruthy 53

4. A Diamond in the Rough 75

5. Starting to Search – pre-Google. 103

6. E Pluribus Unum 121

7. Meeting Mother and Brother 127

8. My Dad or Our Dad ?. 155

9. Driving to see my 'Real' Dad. 167

10. The Horizon moves as you get closer 179

11. Connecting the DNA 195

12. Birth mom and Real mom. 203

13. Connecting the thread to your Children . . . 209

an Adoption Story

CHAPTER ONE

MEET THE BIG APPLE

"A People without the knowledge of their past history, origin and culture is like a tree without roots."

Marcus Garvey

Some stories never really have a beginning nor an end.

Ruth Wilband was a living contradiction in many ways. Born in 1926 and growing up in Saint John, New Brunswick, on the east coast of Canada to Clara, a homemaker, and husband Stephen, a longshoreman, She was a working class girl in a working class burg; quiet yet rambunctious, ladylike yet tomboyish and pretty, very pretty, and petite. Her family was close-knit and large, though some of her siblings did not make it out of childhood. The era was different than today and medicine was not modern nor childbirth easy. For practical purposes, she grew up closest to four sisters and two brothers.

Aubrey was the first born in 1911, followed by Arthur. Agnes, the oldest girl of 15 children, was a prototypical sibling matriarch, dedicated to remaining ensconced in the town of her birth 'til death. There was also Mary, Douglas, and Donna. Following Agnes on the girl side came Mary, Patricia, and Rita before Ruth arrived, on the scene. She was a conflicting counterpoint to Agnes and yet the two remained close forever and ever. The balance of the family followed with Louise, Eddie, Claire, Joe and then Joanie. Agnes was the family's rock and would remain loyal to her siblings in all of their life's adventures, keeping her judgments to herself, difficult as that would sometimes prove to be. Often younger siblings confide in their older or closest sibling, sharing secrets or simply seeking advice.

Saint John was indeed a large city for its place in Canada, and yet it was not a place of glamour, but more a port of call, a center of industry, prominent for its shipbuilding and its fishing, located, as it is, along the north shore of the Bay of Fundy at the mouth of the Saint John River. The bay there boasts some of the largest tides in the world.

The location lent itself to both great port access to the East Coast, as well as for shipbuilding. Ruth's grandfather was a sea captain by trade. The most abundant settlers in the area were called *the Loyalists*, North Americans who remained loyal to the British crown, unmoved by the political concepts of the American revolutionaries. Many left their homes and their properties in the thirteen colonies to migrate to Saint John where some were promised and given land grants by the British government. Today, Saint John still refers to itself as *The Loyalist City.* The people of the area are also loyal, to their friends and families, few venture away from New Brunswick. If they do however, they always 'come home' for holidays or summer vacations to connect to their roots, and enjoy the self-proclaimed 'the lobster capital of the world' in nearby Shediac. There are a couple of well known names from NB, like Donald Sutherland, and Mayer of MGM fame, but for the most part it has a toned down sort of mentality, easy going and relatable.

Some emigrated from the southern colonies, fearful that the day would soon come when their slaves would be taken from them. At that time, New Brunswick allowed them to keep their slaves. Ironically, other blacks found their way to Saint John desiring to be treated as free men, and so they were. Another major group to inhabit the city was the Irish immigrant seeking refuge from the potato famine. Saint John, it seemed, was a place for the displaced, a place with welcoming arms and a tolerance for a variety of social and political viewpoints. Today, there is no discernible overtone of discrimination to any race or visible minority there. Inequities and faults of the past evolved faster than most north american regions, and even the french and english blend seamlessly, unlike the other bilingual province of Quebec. And yet there were some, like Ruth Wilband, who would eventually leave, bored perhaps, a 'free spirit' looking for something new and exciting. The population of Saint John has been in almost constant decline over the course of the past century, despite remaining the largest city in New Brunswick, Canada.

The Wilbands were not a quiet family. They were active and outdoorsy. Stephen, the father, loved to hunt and fish not necessarily for sport, but for sustenance as well as for profit when possible. Ruth loved to swim. Lilly Lake was her favorite swimming hole, a place she would frequent often with friends. Her childhood had its share of bumps and bruises, perhaps more akin to a typical boy's upbringing. A bit accident prone, perhaps due more to here adventurous and risk taking spirit, she once fell off a diving board and broke an arm, and she even once fractured her skull breaking up a fight that one of her younger brothers got into. This was all the more unusual, considering she was smaller than most kids, even most girls her age. However she was tough, very tough when it counted.

It must have been this mental toughness that made her so independent and so unafraid of adventure and change. While Saint John was fine enough for Agnes, for Ruth it proved far too small and provincial; not at all glamorous. No, glamour was what you found in places like New York City and no sooner had Ruth left high school than she set her mind to getting out of Canada and down to the Big Apple.

It was a different era. The world had been at war, many young men were still stationed overseas or were just returning, and because of "Rosie the Riveter," of WWII warplane manufacturing fame, women were temporarily given a bit more free rein with the direction of their lives. Perhaps it was due to this unique historical window that Ruth Wilband was somehow allowed to venture out on her own, not sneaking and slipping past her parents, but openly and enthusiastically packing her things and heading off to the Mecca of all that was dazzling and exciting.

Today, there are many exciting places to go and live, but in the mid-to-late 1940's, there was New York or there was nothing at all. London and Paris were at war and Los Angeles was just beginning to become the west coast behemoth it is today. New York was the center of the universe – Broadway, Times Square, the Copacabana, and the Latin Quarter. If you could make it there, you could make it anywhere.

Ruth and kid sister Louise went first, followed a few years later by younger sister Claire, and finally by baby sister Joan, each doing so as a way of celebrating their emancipation from high school. All four girls were within ten years of age of each other and when together they acted like quadruplets. As wild and high-spirited as the girls were, and as willful as young Ruth had to be in order to pick up and leave for the big city while still in her teens, she was actually considered "the quiet one," usually drowned out by her younger sisters Claire, Joan, and Louise who were far more outspoken. The four shared one common passion: dancing. If there was a chic nightclub to be found, the Wilband girls found it, dancing the night away as often as possible. Being from Saint John, they were open to anyone and anything. It was nothing to them to go out for a night to an all-black nightclub – if the band was hot and dancing was good. Between the four of them, there was always some scheme available to get themselves past the bouncer at the door.

Ruth took her dancing seriously. It was an era of specific dance moves, of tangos and cha-chas, mambos and bossa novas. One did not just get out on the floor and flail about. Ruth knew this and wanted to let it be known she was no hick from the sticks. Some clubs offered dance lessons early in the evening as a come-on to fill the hall and Ruth would be there. During the day, when she had saved up some money, Ruth would also look for studios in Manhattan that offered dance lessons sometimes for a fee, sometimes for free. It was all about pride. If there was some new dance she hadn't quite mastered, then Ruth was damned if she was going to sit that one out. Claire, Louise, and Joan enjoyed dancing, too, but neither took it to heart like Ruth.

There always seemed to be two Ruths. One was the quiet girl who always took stringent care of her looks and her clothing. The other was the joker. The joker, the life of the party, would come out after a few drinks at a nightclub. That particular Ruth had no problem talking to men and sassing back at them as brash as could be. Ironic again, as first impressions would peg her as quiet and reserved.

Time passed. Months turned into years. The girls worked, but most were not what one would call a "career girls," excepting Joan, who did open a business of her own for a time. They earned their keep,

kept themselves fed, put a roof over their heads, and then went out for fun and frolic. One of Ruth's first jobs was in a doctor's office, as was Louise's. The jobs didn't pay much, but doctors were wealthy and when their wives would clear out their closets for new coats and dresses, Ruth and Louise were more than happy to accept the offer to pick through the piles for first choice before what was left made its way to some charity shop. The quality of the goods was stellar and so they were more than happy to be the recipients of this largesse. What they couldn't fit into they occasionally shipped back to their younger sisters in Canada. The Wilband girls back home were thrilled at these gifts, strutting around Saint John in what may have been New York hand-me-downs, but were the best quality clothing in all of New Brunswick.

Ruth had many jobs during her time in New York. One time, she had a job as a coat check girl at a swanky nightclub, once receiving a $100 tip from none other than Frank Sinatra. One such cocktail bar she worked at was called "Proof of the Pudding", which was one of her favorites. Along the way, she also worked in a very high-class women's apparel shop. In each of these jobs she was required to dress well and dress attractively and she did, sinking most of her earnings into fine clothing. Between her natural good looks and her haute couture fashions, Ruth was quite the stunner.

Joan, the brashest of the three sisters, spoke often of Ruth's great luck with men. In Joan's eyes, Ruth always managed to attach herself to men with money, men who would show her a good time and take care of her monetarily so she could dress nicer and live finer than the other three. Unfortunately, having moneyed men around also absented Ruth from having to worry too much or learn much about money management. It was a different era, and men were often in charge of money, while women had their place, quiet and removed when it came to more serious matters.

New York was not a fling for the four Wilband girls, but a new and permanent state of being. Years went by. Wars began and ended. Was there romance? Yes, and lots of it. But the Wilbands of New York were no longer Saint John girls, destined to marry a man before they turned twenty-one, becoming hausfraus as had Agnes, still back in Canada. There had been love affairs, but nothing stable, nothing leading to marriage – at least not right away – and yet there was no weeping over their state of affairs. Life was good, maybe even better than good. For some and for a time, men were interchangeable, not something to be served and waited upon.

Louise was the first to take the plunge, marrying in 1953 after six years as a single gal in the Big Apple. Claire went next in 1955. Joan waited until near the end of the Eisenhower era before she finally wed, claiming herself, "the wiser one to wait." By the sixties, only "Ruthy", as the sisters called her, remained unwed.

But then nature stepped in. Sometime in the fifties, Ruth became pregnant and aborted. Not all the sisters were aware however, as this was a more private affair at the time, especially for a more private woman. In 1962, Ruth found herself pregnant again. The father was an Italian fellow; his name unimportant. Ruth had taken a liking to Italian men, having once spent some time with a certain Nat LaCicero, *aka* Nat Brown, a mobster on the "money-management side", who had been linked to Frank Costello, America's number one gangster in the 1950's, the defacto leader of New York's famed Tammany Hall and Al Capone's successor as the most famous criminal kingpin in America. Ruthy lived with Nat for a while until his untimely passing. The sisters loved telling the story of cleaning out Nat's apartment following his untimely death, and finding multiple false drawers and hidden holes behind pictures etc., each with hundreds of dollars stashed inside. But Nat was gone from Ruth's life by now and this new man was far too transient to her existence for her to want to build a life with him all on account of a biological accident. He had feelings for her, perhaps would have even married her had she insisted or even informed him of her pregnancy, but Ruth simply wasn't feeling towards him the way a woman wants to feel when she agrees to marry a particular fellow.

Agnes. Agnes would know what to do. Agnes, the rock of the family, was still up in New Brunswick. For reasons long forgotten through time, Ruth concluded she did not want to abort this time. Abortion was illegal still, although this did not affect the family planning of the wealthy, for whom everything was always safe and legal. For the working class, though, things were far tougher, though doable. Ruth did not wish to take another chance, though, with the classic "back alley" abortion. She called up Agnes and arranged a coming-home visit.

Arriving back in Saint John, Ruth spilled out her heart and her secret to her older sister. Agnes certainly could not have approved, nor had she ever really approved of her younger sisters' lifestyle in the big city, but still, family was more important than moral judgment. Agnes was married and already had children of her own, but it was soon mutually agreed that Ruth would stay in Saint John until she was ready to deliver and then once she did, Agnes would adopt the child herself, rather than pass it off to a stranger.

It was a sensible arrangement, made better by the fact that all parties involved had vowed to be quite open about it. Ruth no longer cared what the Saint John people had to say about the situation, or her for that matter. She had left them years ago and no longer lived her life to suit them. Thus Stephen, a baby boy named after Ruth's father, was born. Ruth stayed for a short while, but soon was back off to New York, leaving the baby behind. Stephen would grow up with Agnes and her husband, calling Agnes "Mom," but also fully aware that he had another mother and her name was Ruth. This was far more open than most illegitimate births in those days, where in some cases the grandmother would raise a grandchild as her own, and the child would be raised to believe the actual mother was a sister. Such was the case with many, including some famous names such actor Jack Nicholson and singer/actor Bobby Darin. But no such hiding or obfuscation of fact was done in this instance. Ruth would visit from time to time and when she did, the boy called her "Mom" as well. It was an odd arrangement, but a loving one. Stephen grew up surrounded by love and with lots of extended family. He was happy, and wanted for no more than any child.

Two years later, Agnes's niece, Nancy, began coming down to New York for extended visits. Nancy, a pretty, gentle and somewhat less adventurous sole than the Wilband sisters, found all the adventure she wanted in visiting the big apple with the ladies. It was arranged for her to stay with Ruth so that she would not be all alone in the big metropolis. This tickled Nancy to no end, as Ruth treated her as an equal despite a twenty-year age difference. With Cousin Ruth, Nancy was an adult, a big girl now, and Ruth trotted her all over the city like she would any of her other girlfriends. One time a close friend of Ruth's, Norma Scott, visited from Saint John, and Ruth took Norma and young Nancy by subway into Manhattan. For Nancy it was intoxicating – in every sense of the word, first time in the BIG CITY, hearing the sounds of cars and music everywhere. They once walked by a place with the great American Jazz band drummer Gene Krupa playing, and Nancy was so taken with the flamboyant Gene, that Ruth managed to get her into the club to watch one of his sets when she was only 16 years old. Other times they would visit the '1030 Club' together, however young Nancy was never allowed a drink. She did become far too addicted to Coca Cola in the process however. Ruth let her smoke – the big taboo of the era – and Ruth talked her past the front doors of all of the city's "poshest" night clubs. Would that every seventeen-year-old had such an enlivening mentor. Time with the Wilband sisters in NYC was always like first class to a Saint John girl – always as the best : **P**ort **O**ut, **S**tarboard **H**ome.

When Nancy was on the scene, she and Ruth lived on East Ninth Street in Brooklyn, an address Nancy learned to memorize quickly in the event of any emergency. With an ever watchful eye however, Ruth never, ever let Nancy ride the subway alone, or take a cab alone. Through those 16-17 year old eyes, there was no one like aunt Ruth, who she felt seemed to 'have it all."

Around this time, Ruth was not the only unmarried girl to have unwanted pregnancy problems. A very close friend, was between marriages, got pregnant, and chose to follow a different path, deciding to go to Mexico to terminate the pregnancy, and where availability and discretion was more plentiful. So Joan, Ruth, Claire, and Louise decided to make a "supportive" vacation of it, they all trotted off to beautiful Puerto Vallarta together. It made the true reason for the visit a little more palatable and the company of the sisters most certainly helped ease anxieties. They chose a nice resort hotel and lounged by the pool. It was there that Ruth met a man, a very special man, one who caught her gaze and held it. For the entire latter part of the trip, to the dismay of her sisters, Ruth was impossible to find, spending all her days and nights with this new man.

His name was Harter.

CHAPTER TWO

A BOYS ROOTS

"My upbringing made me who I am now. But I can become merry and happy at once. There were many years that I was feeling at a loss about my life or how I grew up. I couldn't understand what is right or what is precious. At that time, I was so miserable and self defeating. I was feeling angry with various things. My anger came up to the surface then. I don't say such tendency has disappeared. Even now there is anger and the dark side in myself. But it is the first time I've been so close to the light."

Johnny Depp

I WAS ADOPTED AT THE AGE OF TWO WEEKS IN SAINT JOHN, NEW Brunswick. Don't ask me too many details about it because I was far too young to remember. I also have a brother, Marcel, who is three years older than me. We are not genetic brothers, for he, too, was adopted in the years prior. Our 'real' parents, the ones who raised us - for who else is one's real parents but the people who raise you and were with you all along life's way -unfortunately could not conceive together. Apparently the adoption experiment with Marcel was considered a success in the early 1960's and so they decided to roll the dice one more time and add me to the family.

Marcel and I both came to my folks via Catholic Welfare, a wonderful organization that made the adoption process a very personal one. Their empathy was evident and my parents claimed they could not have asked for better accommodations and assistance. They told me picking out a child for adoption was sort of like going to a restaurant. They asked you what you were looking for – a boy, a girl, blond, brunette, young mother, older mother, young Catholic mother, what have you, and "assumedly" you got what you ordered. I mean, if you asked for a boy and got a girl, it would be pretty obvious, but otherwise you took all else they told you about the child on faith – no pun intended – and, in the case of my parents, they were happy with what they got.

It's funny, but one of my earliest memories, talking to my mother about how I ended up with her and my dad, was that I was, quite literally, "picked out," as there were a number of babies at Catholic Welfare at the time and they were given a choice. Mom said I looked "the most pathetic," which tugged at her heartstrings. She said it with love and laughter and I took it in exactly that same spirit. Who hasn't had the experience of going to the pound and falling in love with the puppy that looked so sad and disheveled that you wondered whether anyone would ever give him a home? Apparently, that was me as a baby.

I'd been a breech birth. The doctors used "tongs" and my legs were kind of mangled up with scabs and such when she first saw me, which was very shortly after my birth. I was soon fine, once to my new home, as I was during my childhood as well. The truth is, childbirth is traumatic and honestly, not all babies are beautiful. Some of us arrive in this plane of existence looking like something the cat dragged in. Mom still jokes about my feet and my long toes, that they got that long as the doctors "pulled" me out by them. I retort by telling her I wanted to come into this world that way in order to "land on my feet."

Some couples try to find a baby that perfectly matches their physical characteristics. That being said, Marcel and I do not look at all alike, nor do we look like either of our parents. He was dark complected while I was fair. I always had a thick head of hair and still do (albeit graying), while his is now pretty much gone. My mom is cute, short, and at times, like most 'real moms' struggles with her 'weight watchers' attendance. This doesn't really describe neither Marcel nor I really, albeit Marcel can gain a pound or two in the 'off season'. On the other hand, there's always that nature versus nurture argument. Being around whoever is raising you, you unconsciously pick up various mannerisms; mannerisms that suggest to the outside world you are genetically connected. I can't tell you how many times people said to me during grade school, "You look just like your father." Once, visiting Marcel in the hospital after he took a rock to the face, a nurse said "You must be his brother. I can tell." These were, of course, people who did not know I was adopted; strangers, since our family never hid my true lineage from anyone we knew personally. Truth was, by the time I was in my teens I was about a foot taller than my dad, who looked like a little French-Canadian Ronald Reagan while I looked anything but, yet that speaks to my point. Marcel and I picked up a lot of his gestures and facial expressions and people saw it. The funny expressions that embarrass you when your parent's say them when you are young, become the very ones you say around your own children. Those also create a 'linkage' and likeness to adoptees.

My parents were told during the adoption process that my biological mother was 'a young 15 year old girl', which suited them and their sensibilities nicely. From then on, they assumed somewhere out there in the big ol' world was some unfortunate young thing, perhaps still in her teens, who'd made a mistake and luckily they had come along to give that baby of hers a kind and loving home.

Babies being put up for adoption are still given a name by their birth parents. I suppose it's simply because in the time between when they are relinquished and when they are placed it would be inconvenient, and maybe even a little cruel, to refer to a baby as merely, "baby," especially since there are often many of them in the temporary care of whomever is facilitating the adoption. What would they do otherwise, give us numbers? Adoptive parents often then rename the child, and this name makes it to the original birth certificate if adopted young enough. My name, Michael, came from my birth mother, with my original given name on the birth record as first name "Michael," middle name "Thomas." It was the first name that appealed to my adoptive parents and since they hadn't had their hearts committed to some other first name, they simply changed the second to add my dad's Rene; and I remained "Michael" – now "Michael Rene."

By the time I was old enough to be cognizant of what was going on around me, Marcel had already come to know he was adopted. How exactly that came about, I do not know, but it simply was. Thus, since he knew how he came to live in our house and he knew how *I* came to live in our house – I mean, he saw me being brought in – there was never any obfuscation about me being adopted, too. Do I recall some big, formal, "sit down, Son, we have something important to discuss with you" moment? No. I know that may sound strange, but it simply never went down that way. We were never an emotionally dramatic family. Marcel knew (again, I don't know how they handled it with him, but it *had* been handled), and I knew. It was just the way I was brought up to learn who I was.

Mom never minced words. There were no cute euphemisms. I was told I was adopted, I was told what that word meant, and I was told that when I was older if I ever wanted to learn more about my biological parents, she and Dad would never stand in my way. Interestingly enough, other kids in the neighborhood were adopted, too. Some of them were my good buddies. They also knew they were adopted. I cannot recall any case where Mom had to tell me in hushed tones at the dinner table, "Johnny from down the block is adopted but he doesn't know it yet. Don't ever tell him that you know." I suppose it was a cultural thing in my neighborhood. A lot of us were Catholic, thus we didn't support abortion, and if you are going to be against abortion you'd better be in favor of adoption or else you're just a hypocrite.

Looking back, I suppose that adoption is only as big a deal as it is treated. I've heard of people going their entire lives assuming they were natural children and then finding out they were adopted. That really stinks, in my humble opinion. No one should live under the cloud of such uncertainty. Finding out much later in life rocks your world. It's like being a chronically unfaithful spouse. You're a liar, and no matter how much you claim you were trying to spare someone's feelings, you were actually only trying to avoid conflict and deprive another person of the free will to do with the information what they wished to. Of course there are those 'unique' situations where a child was adopted to save embarrassment for a younger family member out of wedlock, but for the 'standard' adoption, it is best the child just know from the earliest days to formulate a healthy self image and forego any dramatic shock of being told later. Some adoptive parents are afraid that the moment they have a conflict with their child, the child will say. "I'm going to run off and find my *real* parents." I believe it's simply best not to candy coat it in anyway, and just tell the child at a very early age. In this way, the adopted parents are viewed as truly having wanted the child all along. This is not always the case for children raised by their *biological* parents, ironically. After that, if there are still threats and problems, all I can say to that is if your kid is that messed up and unhappy to want to "find his *real* parents," you likely had tons of issues you should have worked out long before that utterance left his or her mouth. I never wanted to trade my parents in for some other set of people. These were the people who loved me. This was my "forever home." Why would I think for a second I'd be better off with someone who had already decided they didn't want me?

My parents certainly were secure enough in themselves and brave enough that they never for a second thought they'd ever lose me or my love. Long before the Internet, when everyone's life revolved around the local phonebook, there was a place in the first few pages of every new phone book where you could write down your "frequently called numbers." My mom went through a standard ritual every year when the new one landed on the front deck to translate all the family and friends phone numbers into the pages provisioned in each new book. One of those numbers my mom always wrote on the very first line of this page in each new phone book was some organization called "Parent Finders." Each year, with each new phonebook, Mom would scrawl in that name and phone number. Like I said, it was like a ritual. She knew I could find it, particularly once I was older and was using the telephone more frequently. Without having to make a big, melodramatic scene about it, it was her way of reiterating that if I ever wanted to check things out and find my birth parents, I was welcome to do so, no questions asked. I suppose there was a comfort in that. They say that some people who grow up with food addictions do so because they grew up always fearing they wouldn't get enough to eat, while in other homes if there was always enough food around, they would naturally grow up with more self-control. I suppose it was similar to that. Finding my birth parents was never "forbidden fruit." It was offered up to me so often that frankly, I really could have cared less about ever pursuing anything regarding my biological background when I was young. Marcel felt the same way.

We were not what I would ever have classified as poor. I was aware of those around us in the North end of Canada's oldest incorporated city as being much worse off. I suppose there's no point in trying to dress up our financial status, however. Think *low income* if it suits you better, although "hard working and proud" suits me just fine. I was never ashamed of my parents or my upbringing and never will be. My dad was a laborer who worked primarily in the glass industry as a glazier, installing windows, and large thermal pane frame construction in tall buildings and such. In the early days before he made foreman for larger jobs, he would often be 'on call' for any emergency jobs. He travelled through the week quite often on new projects with compressed deadlines, since *closing in* the building needed to make up for time lost during the other construction trades, and the final construction date standing firm left it up to him and his crew to make up the time. So most of my memories were mom raising the boys, and dad coming home on the weekend for a day or two of rest before heading back out for the next week. The 'on call' situation often pulled him from those weekends also, if a store or bank had a broken window, there was no time to *wait until Monday* to repair it, it had to be done immediately. He liked the overtime, and felt a little privileged at times to be offered the work. For me I often felt bad for him, as there were many times these 'emergencies' would occur on holidays, and a Christmas evening was never off limits either. Dads' work ethic was epic; he very seldom ever shut down. Even when on vacation he was always working on something, for us or a neighbor.

He came from a very large Catholic family in northern New Brunswick, with 11 brothers and sisters. He was one of the three oldest boys and when his father died while they were still school age, the three of them pitched in to hold the family together and support one another. They had to leave school and go into the woods to cut logs for firewood, to make repairs on their home, and to provide fuel for heat. Eventually, they began chopping wood as a job in order to have an income for the family. So he permanently dropped out instead of finishing high school so that the family could be provided for.

My mom who raised me, on the other hand, did graduate from high school. When my parents met, for practical purposes, he could only speak French and she only English. I suppose the physical attraction was obvious, but there have been a lot of family jokes made over the years about how great a marriage can be when neither party can completely communicate with the other. Dad's name was Rene and Mom's was Joan. They met in northern New Brunswick, as Dad's hometown was Acadieville and Mom's was in nearby Harcourt. Saint John was south of where both of them had grown up. To Dad, Saint John was the "big city" where work would be more plentiful. Once they met; it was love at first sight, and he proposed to Mom in a Saint John city park besides the New Brunswick museum, only a stone's throw from the home in which I would be raised, on Alexandra St. As an adopted child, the world you see as you grow builds many of the perspectives that shape your thinking of what life can offer, what relationships are supposed to look like, and to some, life's limitations. Although this is true in many ways, an adopted child also has the imagination of what a parallel life may have offered, and can often remove many limiting thoughts of what is possible in the future for them.

Alexandra Street is a short, dead end street with only 11 houses, on the north end of Saint John. The north end is one of the oldest sections of town. Anyone will tell you that the older parts of most towns are also usually one of the poorest. They're the areas where once the homes begin to go to seed, the people who built them move out to newer developing areas and those settlers are replaced by the poorer immigrants new to the area. Alexandra Street comes off Douglas Avenue, where several ship captains had large homes with separate maid quarters' homes built behind them. Today, most of these large homes are broken up into apartments, with only a couple restored to their original use as single family homes. At the end of the small dead end street that I grew up on was a real rarity in a busy old city, with an undeveloped area just behind it. It was a plentiful 'adventure' areas for kids, hills to climb, apple trees, and even a railroad track to occasionally 'jump a train' and ride to nearby neighborhood and then try to jump off. Occasionally the train would pick up speed and we would not be brave enough to jump off, and on those days the walks home were quite long. Our home, at the bottom of the street, was a modest duplex, vintage 1910, with three stories on each side. My mom lived in one part of the house, while renting out the rest until I finally moved her to a special care home in 2016, and the house sold to a lovely young lady to then enjoy on Alexandra St with her own family.

Saint John was large enough that while you may have known all of your immediate neighbors, people from the other side of town might as well have lived on the other side of the country. It was fragmented. Northern Saint John did not really mix with western Saint John, southern Saint John, and so forth. It had nothing to do with guarded jealousies; it was merely that we were all rather spread out and our school systems were many. Hockey competition was one element that brought cause for trekking to other parts of the city, however.

I don't want to make any rambling dissertations on poverty, but there are all sorts of poor people in the world. We were working poor, and my mom and dad strove to raise us up by our bootstraps, as they say. They were hands-on parents who loved Marcel and me very much. On the other hand, there are the folks who are poor because of other problems – alcoholism, laziness, those wallowing in and choosing to be impeded by their lack of education. They tended to be bitter people who ended up having bitter, angry kids.

Most days when I walked out the door to go to school it was an adventure in self-preservation in neighborhoods nearby. There were times when I fought my way to school and I fought my way back home. I got the sense early on that not everyone experienced the same challenges, as it had a lot to do with the way you looked, the way you walked, who liked you or didn't like you. Sometimes all a gang of misfits needed to 'jump you' was hearing that a girl, whom you may not have even known, was rumored to like you. That seemed sufficient reason for three or four guys to try and bury you in a snow bank. I learned over time to mask as best I could any altercations from others out of embarrassment. Walking out the door could at times mean angling for a fight, whether you wanted one or not. I can't say I ever learned to enjoy fighting, but who among us doesn't enjoy surviving? Anxiety was always high, and I worked hard not to show it. That is, perhaps, a skill I maintain today. But in those days, like many other teens growing up in that old Port City, I fought to survive.

The fighting had an impact on me, but it also had one on my mother, who was not used to such an atmosphere. Me, it was all that I knew, but she'd experienced better and she had such a classically motherly love for Marcel and I that she would flip out whenever I'd come him with a black eye or a bloody nose. She'd fret and start screaming she was going to call the cops, but in places like this, kids punching other kids were the least of their worries. It simply came with the territory and most everyone knew it. Mom never quite got used to that though, so I always knew her as a woman under stress, and I felt a little guilty that I was more often the cause of that stress, although I was never one to go looking for fights. In my neighborhood, you didn't have to; they came to you if you stuck out in any way.

It wasn't as if I was isolated and picked on for one reason or another. It was a neighborhood of battlers and I was treated no differently than anyone else for the most part. Just like society, a few bad apples can give a broader geography a pretty bad rap – as was the case here. So in the same vein, I had lots of pals. The neighborhood, rough as it was, was family just as my mom and dad were family. Nobody was pulling guns on one another or anything crazy like that. It was all just rough and tumble and not much more.

When Marcel and I were both old enough for school, my mother went back to work in order to help our lot in life. Just down the street from us there was a Catholic shelter for battered women and children, as well as unwed mothers, and Mom took a job there. She was the only non-nun in their employ. I suppose it speaks poignantly to her personality. My mother was a natural caregiver who was put on this earth to take care of those who could not easily take care of themselves – a real classic mom. It was fate's cruel trick she could not conceive with my father, but together they found a happy way to deal with that disappointment. She had so much love to give she even needed some extra places to express it once Marcel and I were spending less and less time inside the house. Even after Marcel and I were all grown up and out of the house, Mom continued to work at the shelter with the nuns.

Once I went to university, she took some jobs as a nanny to a couple of families. First, to a family of two doctors for a few years, and also for a while to the children of a member of the Irving family, of Irving Oil fame. Irving Oil is based in Saint John and the Irving family was extraordinarily wealthy. From there she went on to nanny for another family. I don't believe she'll ever fully retire. Today she volunteers for another church-related charity called Saint Vincent de Paul. Again, it is run almost exclusively by nuns, save for my mom and a few others. They eventually had a small ceremony for her where they made her an 'honorary nun', an honor I'm sure she cherishes.

Hockey is the national game of Canada and Marcel and I were normal, stick-banging Canadian boys, so of course we played hockey constantly. We'd play out on the street right in front of our house; the urban Canadian equivalent of hanging a basketball hoop on some telephone pole or garage. Our street had a dead end so we'd pull our goalie nets, such as they were, out into the street and play. When a car came down the road, which, thankfully, was rare given our dead-end location, one of us would yell "Car," and we'd move the nets out of the way and then move them back out again.

Once we reached the age of six or seven, we were signed up for organized hockey, as were all the neighborhood kids. I mean, why get in fights to and from school when you could play the national game and beat on each other legally? Marcel and I were not afforded an experienced hockey-playing dad, and hockey training school was reserved for families with money. So our skills were confined to more natural talents, like speed. Marcel was a more naturally talented hockey player than me. I recall a friend going to a tournament that Marcel was playing in, and asked me what his number was so he could watch for him. I said that I wasn't sure, but if you just 'listen' for the skater that stood out, you'll find Marcel, as you could always hear his distinctive chopping up of the ice when he turned on the speed. I was always in admiration of his natural athleticism.

I speak to Americans who tell me about their experiences with baseball, where they'd join a youth league that would provide balls, bats, catcher's equipment, bases, and even, for the poorest kids, gloves. You couldn't take the stuff home; it belonged to the team, but it was there and it allowed kids of all incomes to participate. In Canada, the younger kids in minor 'house' league hockey were handled the same way. Even if your mom and dad couldn't afford anything for you, even skates or sticks, you could still manage to participate and get by, which was good. In the early days starting out in hockey, buying a full set of gear is quite expensive, so this helped a lot until we eventually got gear of our own. To me, that's the definition of "community." Today, as a grown man, I may go on a bit about how rough the area was, but the truth is, there are some guys from Saint John I've known since I was in kindergarten that are still considered my best friends, and we connect every year at Christmas or summer vacations when possible. I am the godfather to Brian's first child, Dave who lived up the street has come to visit in Dallas, and I see Mike, who lived directly across the street, every other year or so to catch up.

Then there's the high school crew, who when we're together we seem exactly the same for some reason and just enjoy getting together if even only for a "kitchen pass" beer or two. Around our 25th high school reunion, Dave (the jock), Brian (Dobber), Paul (Dogbreath), Chris (Crow), Terry (T' or Wop), Derek (Smitty), and I met at a downtown pub for a few one evening, and it was like we never skipped a beat. Dave was high school all-star athlete, Brian the city's famous actor for local plays, and Chris the high school brainiac. T was always smiling and easy going, Derek was the smiling "reluctant instigator" and jokester, and Dogbreath – well I'll leave that to the imagination. A few good laughs and classic "cameo appearances" of the personalities we all love showed up once again. That's a testament to the kind of place it was, and more importantly the type of people in the 'Maritimes'. We set down roots there of some kind, roots I would hang onto forever.

As we grew older, my brother and I kept up with hockey and did whatever work we could find in order to raise money to upgrade our equipment. I remember when Marcel, who was three years older than me, got his first real job. One thing he did with one of his first pay checks was to buy me a new pair of skates. It was really a selfless act, one that I never forgot - and one that also defined his giving character. Although he and I fought with each other a lot during our younger years, as brothers do, we also looked out for each other when needed.

There was a large flat field nearby where snow would melt and then freeze over. So in the winter, once it got cold enough and retained enough frozen surface, Marcel and I and the rest of the guys from the neighborhood would traipse over with shovels and brooms and we'd clear the snow so we could stop playing in the street and could instead glide upon real ice. We'd play hockey all day and all night, stopping only for school and the occasional meal. Our boots would serve as the hockey net posts, as it was too far from home to carry actual nets. This worked fine, except for chasing the puck into nearby snow banks after scoring slowed the game a bit, but such is the nature of neighborhood games.

While hockey allowed us boys to work off some of our aggression, on other occasions it only fueled the frustration that always seems to simmer in lower income areas. Yes, on the ice you could give a guy a hard check or even throw down the gloves and brawl, but in places like Northern Saint John, it didn't always end once the buzzer went off signaling the end of the game.

Our games were probably rougher than most. Guys often carried their issues off the ice onto the ice. If some group of guys came through your neighborhood looking for trouble on Wednesday, if you faced them on the ice Friday, no one was looking at the score board, if you know what I mean. The game could at times look more like professional wrestling than elegant, well-skated hockey. If some guy was going out with some girl you had your eye on, you'd try to show him up by bloodying his nose whenever you could. Many times, the game didn't always start or end on the ice, either.

For as much as we played a lot of hockey, you rarely heard of guys from our neighborhood making it to the NHL. Moving up in class took money, and we didn't have it. The guys you see on TV usually came from families that could afford to drive them around to more competitive leagues in the bigger metropolis areas, could afford to send them to expensive hockey camps, and could pay for the best equipment and specialized coaching. Compared to those guys, many of us were just a bunch of rag-taggers. For that reason as well, our time spent on the ice was less career-driven. Even at a young age, most of us knew we had no real glamorous future in the game, and so we had no hesitation when it came to playing rough.

For myself, as well as a couple other adopted friends - who I was quite lucky to have in my life to maintain a 'normalcy' to the adopted status, we often would let our imaginations guide our experiences in some ways. I would at times for example imagine that I came from some famous hockey player dad, and my latent skills would soon emerge !. I still smile as I think back about that, as nothing seemed to show any 'step function' in my performance; proving to me that only hard work and experience would provide that progress. It was however nice to imagine, and just the 'idea' can help provide a unique level of motivation for the adopted child. Creatively planted by a clever parent can also help provide some small motivational carrots to add a spark of drive in this way. I often would hear that the best way for an adoptive parent to handle adopted children is to treat as their own biological ones, which I always felt was a fallacy in some ways – in that there are unique needs of an adopted child to be addressed due to the 'unknowns', which biological children do not have. Maintaining the transparency of their adoptive roots should not be ignored in conversation, as they themselves for sure will be thinking about it themselves at times. So an occasional humorous comment of 'who knows if you come from hockey pro roots like Gordy Howe' can provide a unique motivation.

Every once in a while, if you played well enough, you would have a chance to make an all-star team. If so, you got to travel, maybe even stay overnight in a hotel (a big deal for most of us), and play against some of the more serious teams from other areas. We would rarely win such matches, but it was still an honor to be chosen and the trip and the opportunity to play in a nicer arena before a larger crowd was exciting.

One year when I was in my teens, I tried my best but when it came time to pick the all-star team, I didn't make the cut. I was disappointed, as I would often be called to 'play up' a level when they needed an extra player in regular season, but it wasn't the end of the world not making the all-star team however. I hadn't made the team before, but knew even without being able to afford special coaching that I was fast, and I had heart. Somehow I thought the puck handling skills and broader knowledge of the game would magically come to me because of this. One of the beautiful things of naivety I guess.

Coming home from school the day before the weekend all-star tournament, my mother greeted me with some incredible news: Someone had just called and said that one of the all-stars couldn't make it this weekend and I had been selected to move up as an alternate. I was ecstatic. All I had to do was bring my gear down to the local rink Saturday morning at 7AM. We'd be taking a bus to a road game and if we won our first game, we'd even get to spend the night in a hotel. This may not sound like a big deal to most people, and it certainly doesn't sound like much to me today, but at the time, coming from where I was coming from, it was like being selected to go to Hollywood, staying in the finest hotel in town with hot and cold running everything. I'd hit the lottery.

My dad came to see me play all the games he could, but this

particular weekend he had to work out of town to finish a large construction job which he was the foreman for, as he was often called upon to do, and could not attend, much to my disappointment. So there I was on that cold and early Saturday morning, walking down the hill from my house all alone, then following the old railroad tracks for a long trek until I reached the Lord Beaverbrook Rink (LBR) where we always played for our league games. I had my gear thrown over my shoulders and my hockey sticks in hand. It was a heavy load, but I carried it with such enthusiasm that day it felt like a feather. It was later in the season, so while there was still a bite in the air, and you could see you breathe billow out, compared to the weather from earlier in the winter, this was crisp and refreshing air – especially given the excitement of adrenaline rushing through my veins. I would get short waves of this as I walked the long trek along the railroad tracks towards the LBR, and each time a giddy smile would come across my face.

When I got to the rink, approaching from the rear where the tracks passed nearby, I walked around to the front. The front doors were locked. That worried me, but I figured in my excitement I'd gotten there a little too early. I sat on my gear bag against the cold rink wall, waiting for some sign of life to present itself. I thought about how I would get to wear the all-star shirt soon, instead of the transport company shirt from our home team, which excited me even more. Finally, I heard feet coming around the corner to my right where stairs led up from the parking lot. I got up, brushed myself off, and put a big smile on my face. The smile lasted only but a moment.

I recognized the group of four guys approaching me, one of which I'd had a run-in with only a few days earlier. These guys looked like trouble and it suddenly hit me, I had not really made the all-star team – I'd been set up. These guys weren't supposed to be here and no, that call my Mom got wasn't from my coach; it was from one of these guys looking to entrap me. Four on one. Early morning. No team mates around to help me today.

There are surprises in life when you need little conversation to explain what happens next, this was one of those. I stood up quickly and hadn't even made it fully flat to both feet when the first blow hit me to my head and off balance I went to the ground. I scrambled back up to my feet swinging randomly as literally fight or flight kicked in. I fought valiantly for a very brief moment, but four on one is four on one. Pretty soon I was back down on the ground with several legs kicking away at me while I tried to cover up as best as I could. My face was pushed into the snow, and I recall the taste of salt used to help melt the walkway as I struggled to catch my breath. I managed to grab one leg, flipped one guy onto his back, then jumped on top of him and started to wail, but quickly I was then down in the snow being pounded on by three others. My fingers were starting to become numb from the cold when one of them stomped my hand with his steel-toed boots as I tried to get up once. I felt the repeated impact of simultaneous kicks to my body, but one directly to my ribcage left me grasping for any bit of air I could muster to pull in and join that salty mouthful of snow. Very soon I started to feel only defeat and pain.

Finally, some stranger in a pickup truck cruised by on Main Street in front of the LBR. Quickly figuring out what was going on, he slammed on his horn, swerved over, and got out. Being teenagers, my assailants ran for it, afraid of getting into some kind of trouble. The stranger ran over to me and saw how beaten up I was. The old man pulled out a handkerchief and began attending to my bleeding. "Can I give you a lift home?" he asked. Logic dictated I should have taken him up on his offer, but I was feeling more than just physical pain. I was ashamed and embarrassed, not just because I'd been beaten up, but because I'd been made such a fool of, believing I was good enough to have been selected as an all-star, comprehending that my ego and my personal insecurity was such that I could be suckered into walking into such a trap. I was scared, too. What if that man hadn't come along? These guys were playing for keeps. This wasn't just some fight where as soon as the kid getting pounded said, "Uncle," the beating would stop. No, these guys were thugs who weren't going to stop until I stopped fighting back or stopped moving. Even though it was now over, it was scary and it made me hurt all the more.

As dumb an idea as it was, I turned down the stranger's kindness and told him I'd be all right as I got to my feet and started back on my lonesome way along the railroad tracks back towards my home. The walk back towards home seemed a much longer trip that is was earlier in the day, the excitement in my veins was now replaced with a different type of anxiety. I started to feel pains in areas I hadn't been aware I was hit, my ribcage was sore when I breathed in deeply, and I was limping a little from what must have been a kick to my calf. With each step I took, I felt worse and worse; my ego, again, more so than my body. Tears at times welled in my eyes. As I got closer, I dreaded walking back into my own house more and more. My mom would be there and I knew how this would have set her off, especially with Dad being away. She would eventually comfort me, which I certainly needed at the time, after she had a "nervous breakdown," but I was conflicted and torn a bit because I was 15 and becoming a man now. I also knew I hated the feeling I got when I saw her worry, especially when dad was out of town. I was a bit conflicted and confused on how to handle this.

There were woods near our house where we kids would build tree houses in the summer that would last throughout the year. It was a cold day and snow was still all around, but that tree house was still there and so I climbed up to it and sat down inside. I call it a tree 'house', but it was more a platform floor built in a tree, with partial walls, and with only around one third roof coverage from a single sheet of plywood angled to allow rain and snow to slide off and not build up. Still, as rough as the small shelter was, it was a place of quiet contemplation and I stayed there considering everything that had happened to me, and all that was going on in my life at that time. It made me sad. I didn't think of revenge; I thought more of pure, raw, sadness.

Hours rolled by as I sat in the tree house waiting, and I still could not get motivated to move. I didn't want to go home because I didn't want to tell my mother exactly what had happened to me. I wanted my parents to think I could handle myself. My entrée to manhood had been struck.

Finally, I figured enough time had passed to assimilate a trip to the game and drive back to town, and so that I could conceivably come walking home, claiming we had only played one game, which would have meant the bus would have brought us home the same day – no overnight hotel stay for us. I had packed ice on my face earlier to reduce the swelling, and tried to make myself look as best as I could.

My mother was not unfamiliar with me coming home looking like I'd been in a brawl after a hockey game. She asked me for the details, of course, and I made it sound like every other hockey game altercation. I told her, "a fight broke out, both benches cleared, everyone got into it, I took a few punches but I'd be all right." Nothing too much out of the ordinary. Being a mom, she still hovered over me and briefly checked my wounds, cussed me a bit for participating in the violence, but I made sure I played it as if it was nothing out of the ordinary and she seemed to buy it. She wasn't aware of the then football sized purple bruise on my ribs, only the facial marks. To her I'm sure it was just another day in the life of her crazy boys, and she certainly hadn't realized there was more to it, even to this day I believe. I preferred it this way, as my mom was quite a nervous soul, and let things bother her tremendously. So I developed a habit growing up, one that I'm not proud of, where certain things that would cause her to unnecessarily worry would be "left out". Dad would arrive home later that night when I was already in bed, and mom most likely explained to him what happened, as the next day not much was said about it. This was fine with me as I was already trying to forget. I didn't even tell any of my friends until University due to the embarrassment I felt.

If I'd reached a point in my life up until then where I thought the worst of living in my neighborhood was over, this was a stark reminder that it might always be that way and so long as I lived there, I'd have to remain on my guard. It was depressing, but it was simply something to live with. I couldn't just tell my folks to up and move; we couldn't afford it and it wasn't my call to make. I'd been raised to be an independent man who could take care of his own self and so I would, only better.

Years later I recall several conversations with people who never had to experience such things, or in fact never even got into a real fight before, who would almost criticize me for having gotten into martial arts and "liking to watch fights" such as K2 and much later the UFC events so much. It's really hard to explain to folks like that that you really weren't born with the desire to fight, or to enjoy watching such events. I had more than one incident where I was jumped by 2 or more in my neighborhood, somehow that seemed to occur more with me than others. Oddly this was again not something I talked about with friends, as I was constantly trying to avoid thinking about those types of incidents. I always told myself that I just attracted it unsolicited, but over time you come to realize that there must be something about yourself, possibly the way you look, or the way you carry yourself that triggers this in others. So you end up adapting. Odd how 'necessity' drives people to become good at some of the very things they once feared so much in life.

Visiting home from university during one summer, my dad and a bunch of my childhood friends were sitting around a bonfire at my cottage one evening reminiscing. One of them whom I had since shared the "LBR" story, I can't recall if it was Scotty M or Mike G (Bubba), chirped out, "Hey Mike, remember that time you thought you made the all-star team and instead you just got beaten up in front of the rink and spent the entire day sitting in the tree house?" I smirked through the memory of the pain and embarrassment, only because Dad was sitting around the fire also. I'd shared the tale with my friends over the years, but the reason I'd ended that day up in that tree house was to fool my parents into thinking everything went as planned with the hockey tournament. I turned my head slightly to see the expression on my father's face, as I instantly remembered mid-laugh that Dad never knew about what happened that weekend. It wasn't good. As it dawned on him what had actually happened way back then when I was 15, he remained quiet until there was an opportunity for him to excuse himself. He got up silently and left the beach to head into the cottage, all alone.

Eventually, I went back to the cottage to talk to him. There he sat, all by himself, pensive and sad. I asked him what the trouble was and he told me in a voice choked with sorrow how hurt he was that he didn't know about that old incident. It wasn't that something bad had happened to me; it was that I hadn't told him, that I had not trusted him with this secret. It was like a slap in the face to him, perhaps that somehow I didn't trust him with parts of my life; or that he felt he just should have been more aware and wished he could have been there; I'm not sure which. I'd rarely seen him so hurt and I'd rarely hurt him so badly. I never would have guessed he'd feel that way. But this was the kind of family we had. Our house was minimal, but quite full of quiet love. We didn't just care for one another by rote or family name only. We all felt we had *chosen* one another, and that we were a family because we *wanted* to be one, not because we merely felt obligated to be one. One thing an adopted child can always boast, is that their parents for sure wanted them. Not all biological children can necessarily boast that they are in their family by a conscious choice. Not everyone can be guaranteed that. By keeping secrets from my dad however, I had struck him to his core. This never happened again.

> **"One thing an adopted child can always boast, is that their parents wanted them."**

Like most boys, when I was young, I also loved playing war games. In particular, I loved WWII planes. I was totally into building model airplanes. A lot of boys enjoyed that, but I, and a few close friends of mine took it *very* seriously. My older cousin Bernie and a friend Timmy managed to get me interested, and by looking over their shoulders sort of mentored me. It wasn't enough to simply buy a kit and build it, no, no. We had to figure out new and exciting ways to customize the authenticity and realistic look of the planes in order to make them look like they were miniatures of the real thing having been in battle. Bernie, and Timmy were particularly into the WWII-era planes, and thus so too was I, specifically attracted to planes like the Mustang P-51s, Corsairs, Zeros, and bombers like the B-52s and the B-17 Flying Fortresses. I along with a close cottage friend from childhood, Danny, would build them meticulously, paint them very accurately, and then go for customized "accents." We'd do things like first attempt to paint them perfectly, then "age" them a bit, weather them, and give then a few war wounds. For example, we would first paint the plane perfect to the instructions, then add more realistic touch ups to make them look more authentic as if they were once in battle. We would take flat black paint and stream it back on the underside of the wings from where the guns were mounted, so they looked like they'd been fired many times and the smoke residue coated the underside of the wing. We'd also take needles, heat them up red hot with a candle's flame, use them to poke "bullet holes" down the side of the plane, and then ever so carefully dip a little silver paint inside the holes against small brushes of flat black paint from inside towards the back so they'd look like the plane had just been in a dog fight. We'd even get a little macabre at times by digging some bullet holes streamed in a directional pattern along the side of the plane, into the roof of the cockpit, and then dripping some blood red paint onto the little plastic pilot to simulate him having been shot. No detail was too small. Ironically, I made the B17 Flying Fortress a couple times, in different scales. We built shelves in our bedrooms or hallways so we could display them, these trophies of our proud work and ambitious dreams. Basically we did what boys do, became fully engaged in whatever outlet provided the best opportunity to excel at something.

As years went by, our interests then grew from model airplanes to things like pellet guns. Danny's imagination was always looking for a new game. Well, what's a gun without a target? Having moved well into a teenaged phase, we'd take out what was once our pride and joys, our planes, and they were suddenly like last year's calendar – a useless reminder of days gone by. It began with, "Which of these planes is our least favorite?" That poor thing became the first victim of pellet gun target practice. This proved so invigorating that we'd move onto the next least favorite and so on, until eventually we shot up every one of the model airplanes we'd spent so much time and love creating. Such is boyhood.

My mother and father's families were quite large, so obviously there were lots of relatives. And as with all large families, it is difficult to stay close to them all, especially as families spread out, and travel funds and time is limited. As such, while we would occasionally have short reunions with many of them from time to time, there were some that always seemed to go out of their way to remain close, despite the challenges of life. One such family was the "Martins" up in Northern NB in the Rogersville area – with a huge population of 1200! My dad's sister Lucina, who is also my godmother, is married to Elias Martin, and they also have a large family with children both older than me, as well as younger. My aunt Lucina, as well as cousins from mom's sisters side – Dawn and Julie, are a few that have always remained to stay in contact over the years. It is a shame that time does not afford all family relatives to remain close, but very special bonds occur when they do make the effort; bonds I hope to teach my daughter to respect as she grows through example. One thing that doesn't appear to change regardless of being adopted or not, is that family relationships need to be continually worked in order to maintain them.

Another close family was again one of my father's sisters, Aunt Julie, who lived up near Moncton, NB, and in the summers also had a place north of Shediac in Cocagne Cape, which was right on the coast outside of Moncton, about two hours from Saint John. Aunt Julie and Uncle Jacques had a cottage there, and of their children, the closest in age to me were Jackie and Bernie. Jackie was like a big sister in many ways, and Bernie was a great mentor growing up for things like building models and carving swords out of trees and such – which consumed much of our time on rainy summer days. The cape was on the Atlantic Ocean, but the cape itself formed a barrier to the ocean. Aunt Julie's cottage faced away from the ocean, towards the bay formed by the cape. A small dirt road separated her cottage from 6 others that were actually on the beachfront side of the road. It was at this beach that I met who would become a lifelong friend Danny, whose parents' Alice & Roland also had a cottage at this beach. He and his only sibling Maria were also adopted kids, and possibly a reason we all quickly grew so close and still see each other every summer. Directly across from their cottage was their uncle Len and aunt Viola, with their only child Sandra, who eventually became like an older sister to me. Ironically, Sandra is also an adopted child. So to me, as I grew up, being adopted didn't carry any unusual stigma with it, as many of my closest friends were also adopted. This was very coincidental I felt, and it would not be a bad idea for adoptive parents to seek out some similar friends for their adopted children to associate with in their younger years.

> **"it would not be a bad idea for adoptive parents to seek out similar friends for their adoptive children to associate with at a young age."**

My family and I would pitch a tent on my Aunt Julie's property in order to have a little affordable vacation. This eventually morphed into having a pop-up tent trailer hooked to the back of our car, which we would park on their land. We'd spend a few weeks every summer there. This, too, evolved, since once we were there the cost of living was no different than living in our house. Mom didn't work when Marcel and I were small so we began to stay all summer long with my working dad coming up to visit on weekends.

One summer we noticed that the water front cottage directly across the way from Aunt Julie's wasn't getting its grass cut and was starting to look a bit shabby around the edges. My dad suggested we look into it to see what was going on. With a little investigation it was discovered that the owner had passed away and his elderly widow had no desire to hike on out there all by herself. So my dad decided to make a big move – for him.

My dad had approximately $500 to spare as down payment when he walked into the bank and took out what he described to me as "the largest loan of his life at the time": $3500. He visibly suffered to make this happen, but he knew how happy we would be, creating precious memories and spending summers at that cottage beach area. He bought that cottage, a waterfront property, for a whopping $4000. Today, some of those same little cottages on the shore easily sell for 40-80 times that, so Dad's investment was rather astute. Following his demise, it was passed along to me as the care taker, that little cottage on the Atlantic Ocean's Cocagne Bay, and to this day I look forward to very little, more than I do in getting back there every summer for a couple weeks' vacation. I have since added onto the little cottage a fair bit, doubling the size and with lots of small comfort adds, as well as investments in the waterfront to prevent water erosion, yet it still remains very quaint and true to its original spirit on the Cocagne bay. The cottage beside us came up for sale in 2015 by the DesRoches Family who owned it as I grew up, so I purchased that as well to have for family and friends overflow during summer vacations, as well as for a small rental property.

Fishing boats & traps in foreground.

There was lots of fishing to be had, but the real activity for people up there was lobster fishing. What most people refer to as "Maine lobster" is also New Brunswick lobster due to the wider coastal area for lobster fishing, and I've debated Maine "down-easters" on that point a few times since my childhood. If living in the US, you would think Maine is where 'all' lobster comes from.

'Lower middle class' has its own idiosyncrasies wherever you go in this world. The most my dad ever made in his life was probably less than $45k a year, which he needed to work an awful lot of overtime to achieve, and it was the late 90's before he retired. We sort of lived hand-to-mouth from what I could tell, yet I always seemed to get what I really needed - always. Despite income level, we managed to feast on lobster throughout the summer months. How? Why? Well, for one thing, up at the summer cottage – a modest set of structures despite what they sell for today – everyone had a trade. One guy would be a carpenter. The fellow across the road may have been an electrician, another a fisherman etc. All working people, all tradesmen.

Back in the day, everyone used to help one another and "trade trades." It was kind of the lower and middle class eastern Canadian way. The lobsterman might need new windows. If so, my dad, the glazier, would come down and set him up with brand new windows, expertly installed. Suddenly, our diet consisted of lobster, lobster, and more lobster. Dad had bartered. Neither man had an extra penny to spare, but everyone had something that someone else needed. If an older cottage sat on rail road ties instead of a proper foundation, there was usually a mason somewhere nearby in the neighborhood. So that's how one got a foundation, so long as you had a skill to trade. As well, if there was not a specific tradesperson available, everyone would chip in a hand to make what was needed. It was seldom that money every exchanged hands.

Every other person was a lobsterman in the area, we were *always* getting tons of lobster as dad worked the 'social network' of his time. No Facebook then, just a lot of face time and elbow grease. Growing up, I actually never knew lobster was all that big a deal. For us, lobster was what macaroni and cheese was to other kids. Lobster was so plentiful; my mom would on occasion de-shell lobster and freeze the meat in mason jars for later in the year when it would be out of season. During the summer months however, we'd typically boil it up and then stick it in the fridge. Many people in 'cottage country' have a separate fridge in their shed to keep cooked lobster, and of course beer. Most times we'd just eat it cold, the true east-coast way, albeit unfrozen, just like people eat cold shrimp.

Mom would have the fridge stacked full of mason jars of lobster, ready to eat. When we'd go back to Saint John to go to school in the fall, our daily school lunches would at times consist of lobster sandwiches, meat mixed with mayonnaise on bread or stuffed into a hot dog bun. I distinctly recall at times even being embarrassed by it, not really understanding how special it was. I would look around at the "rich kids" things like eating roast beef or peanut butter and jelly, recalling once that I was "stuck" with lobster again. At that age, I had no frame of reference. I knew we weren't loaded, and I knew that people would at times pay my dad in lobster, which to me meant that lobster was good but something just a baby step above bologna in my mind at the time. Boy did that perception change over time.

Even today, decades later, the idea of going to a restaurant and ordering lobster would never occur to me. And the prices! Who would ever pay $25 to $45 for a single lobster meal? Heck, there would often be times when we'd eaten three or four of them a day during summer months at the cottage. Looking back, I felt that I would have had to have been a Gates or a Buffett to live like that anywhere else in the world, paying restaurant retail prices. Craziness.

These days, when we visit the family cottage, we either go down to the wharf and see the offspring relatives of a fisherman my dad knew named Sniff (who I seem to recall was missing a finger or two), or if in a hurry drive around the Cape to small Seafood store set up in a family's garage only 5 minutes away. If we go to the wharf directly, we would hand the fisherman a bucket of our own, he would weigh it empty, then he'd fill it with live lobster, weigh again, charge six bucks or so a pound for the delta.

I would then take the bucket, bring it back home, take a large propane heated pot outside, fill it with water and rock salt (or water direct from the bay which my daughter now likes to fetch), boil away, stick in the live lobsters, wait 'til they're bright orange, pull them out, turn them over, let them cool, eat what we can, and put the rest in the fridge. Our "lobster fridge" is the same one we've always had at the little cottage – a 1932 General Electric, a square box with a big round motor on top that works like the first day it was brought home. It even has a foot pedal so if your hands are full you can step on the pedal and it will open for you. It came with the cottage and it will probably outlive *me* for sure.

In my youth, I attended the local Catholic school, St. Malachy's, which started as an all-boys school but went co-ed shortly before I entered. It was a competitive place known for providing a good university prep education. Because of that, most all the kids who went there were bound for college. I'd always done well in my studies and also knew it was a place I needed to be. I knew it would be a financial burden to rely solely on my parents, so I also had that as a key motivator. Education was a way out, a way to better myself and live a finer life than they had achieved.

Athletically, St. Malachy's High School was known for hockey (naturally), as well as soccer and rugby. Likely best known for hockey however, as the rivalry was always great with the other local high school Saint John High. SJH tended to dominate in football at the time, as it was a much larger school and with that also came more expensive programs for football. Hockey being the niche for St. Macs was always a bit of a mystery for such a small school. We tended to attribute it to the 'spirit' of ESSE QUAM VIDERI our school motto. We also were blessed with great coaching as well.

Our high school was a great Academic standard in preparation for University, and many Universities recognized that through various scholarships offered to students there with top marks. For the various student activities and team sports trips, we often found creative ways to drive fundraisers to finance trips that larger schools participated in. On one such occasion, friends Paul, Dave and I spearheaded selling tickets to raise money by getting our hands on a new hot trend just started at the time "Cabbage Patch Kids". We waiting a huge line one morning before a large store opened, and Paul ended up "diving" to grab one of the last ones. We raised a huge sum of cash on that one doll to help supplement a big hockey trip to Ontario one high school year.

High School Fund Raiser.

Not having a lot of money sharpens the mind and makes serious one's endeavors. It was fairly innate to me that if I didn't work hard and study hard I would not be able to attend university, and so I dedicated myself right from the start in order to thank my parents for their investment in me. I was a bit of an anachronism. On one hand, the frequent street trouble tapered off into high school days and I eventually put up the tough guy's front to help me get by. On the other hand, once I was sitting in class, I was a "disguised nerd," the bookworm doing what I had to do in order to achieve. I was lucky to have some friends who were well off financially, and actually learned a lot of good study habits from them during my high school days. During exam time in my final year of high school, we would often go to the local University library to study together, sometimes in group level study rooms, other times in private cubical areas, dependent on the topic. This also gave a nice flavor for what college life would be like.

One of the tougher aspects of a working class kid pulling himself out of the old neighborhood was figuring out the ways of the world. The thing is, your parents can hit you with all the typical homilies of, "Stay in school; work hard." But as you age, you need more than that. You need more specific advice and you need direction. All the potential in the world is wasted if it is not directed. The more wealthy and educated families know this. The problem with the working class is that they have no one to really turn to. Your parents are limited to saying things like, "be a doctor," or "be a lawyer," for those are the most educated people they know. Outside of that, they often don't really know how wealth beyond basic salary is made.

I always liked math and science and I always liked to tinker, taking things apart and putting them back together, building things. At some point, someone must have said, "Look at him; he's a little engineer," or, "Michael's good at math and sciences, looks like an engineer to me." Who said it? When did they say it? I have no idea, but it stayed in my head long enough for me to look it up and realize an engineer was something other than the guy who drives a train. At this time, being adopted and not knowing anything then about my birth parents, I felt I could possibly come from a great lineage and have some unique latent undiscovered talent. To me I always felt not knowing my biological parents background, and perhaps their limitations, was somehow a wonderful advantage for me. Unlike most non-adopted kids, I didn't have to look at those raising me and automatically assume their shortcomings, didn't have to live up to certain standards, and didn't have to accept any commentary on my potential. For me, my potential was whatever I could dream it to be. I could envision my own desires, desires not planted by overambitious parents, were all possible and perhaps the very strengths of my unknown and mysterious genealogy. What a wonderful gift for an adopted kid, to not be saddled by someone else's desires and expectations, not limited by known shortcomings of their parents 'DNA', to follow their own initiative and imagination without limits. If only all children had that opportunity.

> **"What a wonderful gift for an adopted kid, to not be saddled by someone else's desires and expectations, not to be limited by known shortcomings of their parent's 'DNA' ..."**

Still, it was far too vague and distant for me. Engineer. I knew no engineers. There seemed to be none in my neighborhood. I certainly felt it would be an obvious advantage to take to someone knowledgeable about this profession. By the time I entered 10th grade, kids were discussing future plans, particularly the kids who intended to attend university. I had to get a better handle on things.

I opened up the phone book. The Internet was just a twinkle in the world's eye at this point in history, but we still had that big yellow book. I looked up "engineers" and found the company closest to where I lived. I put my sneakers on and hiked to the place, walked in the front door – no appointment, of course – and asked to speak to an engineer. The receptionist was taken aback, looking at me like this was some sort of kid's prank, but I was stone serious. "Talk to an engineer about what?" she asked.

I was simple and to the point. "I just want to speak to an engineer about being an engineer." It wasn't much of an answer from where she was sitting, but to me it made all the sense in the world.

There was a fellow standing behind her using the photocopier and he began to chuckle at my brass. "Let me handle this," he said to her, then turned to me and invited me back into his office. Once I was settled, I reiterated my plea. "I just want to know what engineers do."

He stroked his chin and then went into as good a dissertation as he was capable of providing. He told me what he knew and what he did. It wasn't a classic overview. It wasn't meant to be a recruiting pitch as he certainly didn't represent the academic arena, but it made the field come alive for me in a real, concrete way. Suddenly, it was no longer a mystery, this engineering thing. It was a job and here was a guy who did it. He seemed happy at what he did. He wore a nice white shirt and tie, yet he wasn't some fussy paper pusher who couldn't change a flat tire if he got one. I liked this guy. I was able to imagine myself going to work each day and doing the sorts of things he did. All this to understand what an Engineer did day to day. Kids today have no idea how lucky they are to live in the world of Wikipedia and the internet. Suddenly then, I had a kernel of a plan on how to pull myself up and get myself out of northern Saint John and make my parents proud.

During my high school years, staying busy with Rugby, Hockey and Soccer helped to keep me out of trouble somewhat. Girls landed on the radar, and certainly that was a fun discovery. Not having much money, nor a car to drive as dad mostly had company trucks, limited me a bit in my mobility to pursue that classical boyfriend-girlfriend venture. As such "proximity" played more a driver on the romance front. Plenty of 'crushes' of course, and lots of young romance, but generally remained mostly single throughout high school. I really had only one true heartbreak during my high school years, which albeit a short courtship, would be considered my only true 'girlfriend' during that time period. It became my first experience with that all-consuming feeling of how a woman, ok a girl, could command your heart as well as make you do really stupid things in pursuit of gaining hers. That first feeling of love never leaves your heart.

Eventually, my scholarly pursuits paid off and I was offered a few academic scholarships. I graduated 11th in my class and had about 4 or 5 schools offer me scholarships in engineering. Like a lot of lower-income kids, I went to the school that offered me the most money, which ended up being a free ride on a full academic scholarship, contingent upon me keeping up my grades. I also received in addition a soccer scholarship as well that gave me some extra money for books, 'extra-curricular activities', and such.

I played sports all the time as a kid and I would admit to being athletic, but sports, to me actually, was always more of a way of life than a career goal. I was blessed to have amazing coaches along the way to help supplement advice, encouragement and skillsets that parents can often not provide. Lou Simon was that for hockey, and Ronnie Barry for Rugby. Lou was a true hockey staple in Saint John for many years, as well as the father of my good friend Dave – so he sort of provided an alternate parental figure as well for me. Ronnie was one of those uber-cool coaches in high school that always seemed to be able to draw the best out of each player. He was a true player-coach, and ran plays, exercises and tackles along with the team every practice; a true inspiration in many ways with his "to the point" guidance. I was no better at soccer or rugby than I was at hockey, but if someone was willing to give me an educational opportunity because of sports, that was fine with me. I had no delusions of being a professional athlete nor was sports ever the center of my life. Very few boys with athletic prowess have that issue so together in their minds at a young age, but I was always pretty well grounded. I knew I wanted to pull myself out of northern Saint John and instead of relying on something as subjective and flighty as sports or entertainment, I felt math and science were my way out, along with the untethered vision of what my imagination could lead me to believe I could do.

Ironically, I ventured back home to Saint John for a long weekend at the beginning of my freshman year of University, played an alumni rugby game, blew my ACL in my knee out, and would never play a game of University soccer. It was just as well for me, as I was nowhere near as talented as the guys in the lineup, they were all classically trained athletes, and I'm not sure if my high school coach ever really played the game himself, albeit he was ten times more athletic than most my teachers there, and was a great help in providing basics. But my first university, UPEI, still allowed me to keep my athletic grant, which was quite decent of them. Some players however, although far more advanced in their skills than what I had developed and learned in my small hometown remained close friends and roommates. One of my first year roommates,

Alan, was arguably one of our Nations best players, just an amazing athlete. Another roommate Jean-Francois was the goal tender, a French Canadian from Quebec, who seemed to have the mysterious Frenchman persona down to a T. Another close friend and player Peter "Raw" as we called him was also an amazing athlete, could run for days and had mad skills like another Quebecois peer named Richard Pierre-Gilles, who was quite possibly the most athletic guy I ever met up until then. His legs, built only from soccer, looked like they were Greek Adonis carvings. Richard, or "RPG" as I call him, remains a close friend as well even today, and visits the cottage with his family on occasion.

The whole first year was a wild ride for me, as I'm sure it is for many 'first time from home' kids. As I lived in the 'co-ed' apartment style residence on campus called 'Blanchard House", those who played on an athletic team got first choice to the rooms. On my floor were primarily the soccer and basketball teams – both male and female. So I quickly made friends with a couple guys from the basketball team as well. Two guys I connected with first were Joe P and Derek. Joe was black, and Derek was also black but much lighter skinned, so we became known as the "three shade crew" around campus. It is usually in those initial years of University that you pick up nick names, based on something unique or "stupid' that you did. A couple of the basketball players who couldn't pronounce my last name affectionately started to call me "Duey", as that was somehow the best they could muster. I guess handling the French pronunciation of 'Doiron' is not the easiest for the English tongue, so I suppose this is why Joe Patterson decided "Duey" was a better fit. And when a six foot, seven inch black man named Tyrone wants to call you Duey, your name quickly becomes Duey. Another 'clique' I was in on the Engineering side, included Peter from the soccer team, and a local Island boy named Thane. The three of us liked to think we were the cooler geeks in our engineering class, however we likely couldn't have made it through without the help of many classmates like Keith "I don't study and still get straight A's", and Brian 'the Link", a cartoonist and all round amazingly nice guy. The whole class was very small, and all quite special. Today I am still in contact and

close to Thane and Joe, and 'facebook' friends with the Link. Others have
tapered off to their own lives in separate directions. I see Joe whenever I
travel to Toronto, and Thane when I hit the east coast PEI. As for other
nicknames, Joe was 'baby-face", and Thane was "Iceman". I may be the
only guy still referring to them as that however. Three of us had picked
up nicknames following an Annual Engineering Ice-Curling tournament;
Peter "Curl", Mike "Rock", and Thane "Iceman" – which we managed to
commemorate on custom shirts some 30 years later at the yearly cottage
get-together.

Although I blew out my knee in my first year, still I continued to
keep active, developing my body as well as my mind. Having to be in a
soft cast for a few weeks, I started going to a Gym more, as part of the
physical therapy. This got me more and more interested in becoming a
Gym-rat for a time being as a way to channel my energy while my knee
recovered. This then became a fairly large interest for me for a couple

years, working out for hours a day. The summer following my first year at University I even lived in a Gym, literally. It was owned and run by a couple of friends in my hometown. "Scotty and Todd" were local entrepreneurs that had not only a Gym of their own, but also ran other businesses like Gas stations and convenience stores. For their age, they were clearly the youngest business owners I knew. They became pretty good friends, and also provided a great inspiration for me. Scotty and I developed a close relationship, and stayed in close contact through my University years, getting together during summers and sorted road trips. As I moved to Toronto, contact eventually tapered off to a couple times a year, then eventually only during the summer vacation to the cottage. Later, we might never talk at all during the year, yet like clockwork every summer I'd get the call, "Mikey, Scotty here. When are you heading to the cottage?" I would reply with an arrival day, and he said "Bubba, Dobber, Danny, Melanson and the boys coming?" I would reply yes on 'the annual regulars' for the cottage retreat, and give a date, and the conversation was over. And with that, the Swiss clock would click, and my half brother would arrive the day after I got there, every year. Everyone loves Bubba, he's the salt of the earth. Dobber is one of my oldest friends from childhood. Gary was as reliable as the day and night, always there, always having your back if any issues, and to this day still one of my very best buds. This was just the kind of people you find in the east coast, they'll always cherish time with old friends, regardless of how connected you may be during daily life.

Over some time Scotty and Todd sold off their Maritime businesses, and moved away to other ventures in the US, but I do value the friendship we had at that time as it provided my first taste of having to "be responsible", as well as the friendship itself. Some years slipped by without contact as they settled with starting new families. We then connected again and I was wonderfully surprised to hear that Todd became a Minister, and Scotty's family grew quickly to three kids. We will reconnect again and share life war stories, and it will be as if we never skipped a beat.

I then got interested in Tae Kwon Do after later getting to know a friend Randy who was a black belt in Ju-Jitsu. It was fun and it proved good for my concentration. Of course, it's not exactly a gentle sport, and I ended up doing much more when I finished University, breaking many bones, some like my wrists more than once, in this pursuit. I also ended up having multiple shoulder surgeries later in life as more longer term injuries emerged from the sport, which was back then starting to evolve from individual fighting disciplines only, into what was in the early 90's starting to be known as MMA or 'mixed martial arts'. We didn't really give it a name at the time, as it was more just an interest in learning the best elements out of different styles for us then, where as today it is a specific discipline to train in with the popularity that the UFC has brought to martial arts in general. I suppose injuries were inevitable, as I was also at little of a cultural disadvantage – as native Canadians, try as we may, are usually never quite as quick in martial arts as Koreans peers in the DoJo. Now had we gotten them on skates out on the ice …

Earlier in my initial educational pursuits, my dream had been to go into engineering, in particular aeronautical, via the Air Force, which would also have taken care of the educational expenses involved, but I soon found out before leaving high school that 'perfect vision' was then required to be a pilot, and mine was nowhere near good enough. Heck, I was prescribed glasses in high school just so I could see the blackboard. That was crushing for me. What boy doesn't dream of designing jet engines, or better yet, piloting a fighter jet. But it was not to be.

I thought back upon that engineer who had been so kind to me when I was totally in the dark about what sorts of things engineers did. I decided I could be happy doing the kind of work that fellow did all day long, even if it didn't involve flying an F18 fighter, or setting world piloting records for supersonic flight. Perhaps the supersonic flight thing would come later and in a different form such as engine design, but this was the front door, the way in. I was about to become an engineer.

From UPEI I received a Diploma in Engineering in the 80s with a focus on Physics and Math. From there I went onto the University of New Brunswick for a B.Sc. degree in Mechanical Engineering, with a minor focus on Nuclear Engineering as they offered a couple courses on that also. Finally, I got a Masters in Engineering at the University of Toronto with a major in Mechanical Engineering and minor in 'computer integrated manufacturing'. I had now left the old neighborhood forever, on my own terms, and may even be a help to my loving parents. The world awaited me.

CHAPTER THREE

HARTER AND RUTHY

"All difficult things have their origin in that which is easy, and great things in that which is small."

Lao Tzu

Harter Barnes Hull II was born in Waterloo, Iowa April 9, 1924. As a young babe he lived with his family in Memphis, Tennessee and Baltimore, Maryland, until finally settling in Des Moines, Iowa. His father's name was Harter as well. The family was wealthy and quite well established. Going back generation upon generation, the Hulls were lawyers and judges and other prestigious positions within their community.

Harter's great-great grandfather had a large plantation in what is now Uniontown, Maryland in Frederick County. From another branch of the family came great-great-grandfather Edmund Augustus Boyer, had over a hundred slaves that were originally owned by *his* father. Stories tell how he entertained generously and had tutors from Baltimore come live on his estate in order to teach his children. Dancing masters were also on call. For their dining pleasure, oysters were brought out and kept alive in a tank in the basement in salt water; one could on occasion hear them snapping in their shells.

Great-grandfather Boyer, son of Edmund Augustus Boyer Sr., went to private school in Baltimore and then onto medical school in order to study surgery in what most likely has become the modern-day Johns Hopkins University Medical School. He also studied abroad. His father eventually contracted a fatal illness and in his waning days sold the plantation, moved up to Pennsylvania, and then decided to free all of his slaves. He was the first in the area to ever do such a thing at the time. He eventually ended up in Tiffin, Ohio, where he died in 1835.

Young Dr. Edmund Augustus Boyer Jr. moved to Wolf Lake, Indiana, where he married Mary Rebecca Wiley and practiced medicine. Hearing that Native Americans had been driven off of the fertile lands of Iowa, they moved there, moving about depending upon what areas were free of land-war conflict, eventually settling in Oskaloosa, Iowa. There, he purchased around 100,000 acres around the Des Moines River.

On his mother's side, Harter's mother's family included the prosecuting attorney of the southern district of Iowa, who eventually became the state's attorney general for eight years before going to Congress during the McKinley administration. He retired as a US federal judge.

In the town of Oskaloosa, Iowa, founded by Nathan Boone, youngest son of Daniel Boone, one of Harter's uncles originated the Oskaloosa Saddlery Company, which employed many people and was a well-established brand for many years, holding many of the patents used in today's saddles. A grandfather of Harter's also founded the county bank in Oskaloosa.

Young Harter's father went to the University of Iowa, studying structural engineering, and then went on to the University of Illinois, attending their School of Commerce, what one might refer to today as a business school. Young Harter's father got involved in sales, specifically automobiles. Cars were still a bit of a niche item back in the teens and twenties, so one could say he got in on the ground floor of the mass production and mass ownership of what every american family would someday own. He worked for the Sears Motor Company (now defunct), then the Ford Car Company, started his own business as the Harter B. Hull Co. (Dodge Brothers & De Soto line) and a few other roles before moving up to the vice-presidency of the then newly formed Automobile Trade Association, as well as the VP of the National Automobile Dealers Association. One obituary indicated that he was in line for the presidency when he died very prematurely at the tender age of 38; yet still acquiring a full and accomplished life for such a young man.

Harter's father was everyone's definition of the great American success story. Local small-town Des Moines papers followed his exploits, and even his most banal vacations and party-goings were chronicled daily. For the area, the family, quite simply, was high society.

On one of the family's much ballyhooed European vacations, Harter the Elder contracted what, at the time, was referred to as a "blood-related disease," which, in modern parlance, could mean any one of a dozen different things. Nonetheless, medicine of that era was nothing like what we have today and he was unable to recover, thus his premature decline and death.

His wife, Claire, was quite well-educated; again, something rather unusual for the early part of the 20th century for a Midwestern woman or an American woman, period. She attended three different colleges and attained a number of degrees, matriculating at, among others, Grinnell College in Iowa, today regarded as one of the top twenty liberal arts institutions in the country. Unlike Harter, Claire lived well into her nineties.

Harter the Younger grew up feeling the pressure of being the son of two very accomplished people, particularly his father, who rose to such prominence, wealth, and social position at such a young age. He grew to be a tall, handsome Midwesterner, standing around six foot three with a stocky, muscular build. He spoke with a gruff voice, full of self-assurance and at times downright cocky. Yet this 'edge' was often softened to immediate acceptance with his natural born charm. Upon graduating high school, his first move was to attend Iowa State University in Ames, Iowa, where he played football until a knee injury sidelined his athletic aspirations. From there he enlisted in the military, something to set himself apart from the exact path his father took. He went to Canada and earned a pilot's license – a "quickie" way of getting certified and something far easier to do back in the 1930's and '40's than it is today – even before joining the Army Air Corps (AAC), the predecessor to the modern US Air Force, and flew in World War II, part of the time as a pilot while other times serving as a tail gunner, mostly serving on the B-17 "flying fortress," a four engine heavy bomber that wreaked more havoc on Nazi Germany than any other Allied plane.

Harter's Canadian training may have helped to fast-track his wartime service and helped get him the assignment he so sought – the action of doing battle in the air above Europe.

Harter B. Hull II.

The movie *Memphis Belle* is a wonderful chronicle of life on an Allied B-17 during WWII, including its observation that planes and crews aimed for the magic *twenty-five missions* mark that earned them the right to go home victoriously. Unfortunately, not only did most not live to achieve that watermark, some crews actually ended up even serving longer and running even more than twenty-five missions due to the necessities of the extended war. Harter and his crew did 38 missions on a B-17, an incredible stint of wartime bravery and service to their country.

Just like *Memphis Belle* all B-17 crews named their planes, and the naming was quite the controversy, as each man loudly lobbied for his personal choice of moniker, usually something to do with a woman, such as a wife or girlfriend from back home. Harter primarily served on the B17 unofficially known as "Hell 'N Gone," which was his last plane during his wartime duty, mostly as a tail gunner. The "Hell N'" was a play on words, as a woman named "Helen" was the sweetheart of one of Harter's crewmates. The protocols were that men would be shifted from duty to duty over the course of their service in order to keep them fresh and keep them from burning out or stressing out.

Harter served in the famed 487th Bombardment Group, America's first group to cross the Atlantic in squadron formation and first light bombardment group to engage the Nazis. They assembled as a crew in Lincoln, Nebraska before being dispatched to Rapid City, South Dakota. After flying and training together for several months, they were sent to Kearney, Nebraska, where they were assigned to the 8th Air Force in Europe.

The Nebraska days were wild times for the young Harter. One day, part of their training involved flying their newly issued B17 over the rather newly-minted Mount Rushmore. One of the four presidents immortalized there must have rubbed Harter the wrong way, as he began strafing towards the national monument with a 50-caliber machine gun. It was all in good fun, mind you, but it got him a reputation as a little of a wild and crazy guy nonetheless.

On July 5, 1944, Harter and his crew departed for Europe, taking a bounce off several interim locations for other training and connections. Landing first in Newfoundland, Canada, where numerous military bases had sprung up almost overnight. These sleepy little towns suddenly prospered and Newfoundland girls, swept off their feet in all the excitement, married American servicemen by the score. From there it was onto Greenland, then Iceland, and then finally Wales.

In Wales, the crew was temporarily relieved of their aircraft as they traveled by rail to their final base station in Lavenham, England. It was there, in Great Britain, that these young enlisted men truly formed a bond. They were quartered together, five enlisted men to each crew, in mission huts holding numerous other crews. As other crews finished their tours and went back home, for a time his was the only crew still bunking together in their hut, still awaiting their first combat assignment. The officers, of course, had their own, finer quarters.

It was in England where the crew tried to settle upon a name for their plane. Staff Sergeant Harter B. Hull had his own favorite, "Peg O' My Heart," however "Hell "N Gone" is listed in some 8th AF 487th books as the 'nicknamed' 487th B17. It was typical for the men to try to utilize the name of their current sweetheart. Harter had actually gotten married immediately before going overseas, as was common during wartime, and his first wife's name was indeed Peggy. Harter and Peggy had met at a Junior High at dance class, and were married the month after Harter turned 20 – Peggy 19, on May 25, 1944. Looking like the classic WWII flying ace, he also had the requisite leather flying jacket. On the back he also had custom embroidered, "Peg O' My Heart," as a tribute to his hometown honey waiting back in the States. "Hell N' Gone," meanwhile, flew missions to every major battle zone except for Frankfurt. Harter's first love and first wife bore him two children, a family they started some 10 years after marrying. Harter's bomb group, the 487th, had their major site objectives as oil refineries and armaments factories.

The many missions Harter's crew flew on were not all successful, a couple resulting in their B17 taking heavy artillery and flack damage. One such hit resulted in the belly-turret gunner getting shot out completely. This weighed heavy on the crew, as the long flight home in the un-insulated fortress would now also have a large opening in the belly to welcome in the frost, while they mourned the loss of a fellow crew member. Reminders of their mortality were left to view on the inside area of the turret cockpit, bloodied and now empty as a memory of how quick one can go in the game of war.

Just as his father had once been the darling of the local Des Moines newspapers in his day, so too, now, on a smaller scale was young Harter, the much-decorated WWII veteran who had received his 8th Oak Leaf Cluster among other decorations. Once he returned to a hero's welcome, he gathered together some additional schooling in engineering and business. From there he turned to the insurance business, where he showed the same acumen for selling as had his father before him. Harter was a 'people person', a charmer, and could talk an Eskimo to buy pallet blocks of ice. He could flat-out sell.

Harter B. Hull II.

Harter sold for others at first, then formed with a partner his own company, which eventually established as even larger company still in existence today named Brokers Clearing House, a nationwide insurance concern. In many ways, Harter had the best of all possible worlds. He came from money, but driven under his own ambitions primarily, and yet he could also point to accomplishments of his own. The end result, though, was eminently prosperous – Harter B. Hull II, as had been his father before him, was a wealthy, successful man. Still however, filling the shoes of his father remained a lofty goal to Harter, oftentimes feeling he could not quite reach Harter Seniors' stature in life.

It was by pure happenstance that Harter was in Puerto Vallarta, Mexico during a 2 yr separation period from Peggy, that same sunny day as Ruth Wilband and her sisters back in the 60's. Life is like that. Was it typical for Harter to run off with strange women on a whim and an opportunity? Who knows? Gentlemen never say and gentlemen then were discreet enough to cover their tracks. Harter Hull, in that sense, was a gentleman. And he always made a woman feel like a million bucks.

The Wilband sisters were somewhat insulted that their older sister Ruth, instead of staying with them in Mexico, ran off with some strange man, but there was suddenly no Ruth around to express their displeasure to. It seemed as if the Ruth and Harter met and then disappeared for the entirety of the trip, days and nights without checking in with anyone. Under other circumstances it would have been romantic. In the eyes of Harter and Ruth, it was most indeed romantic. But to the rest of the world, including Ruth's own family, it was scandal.

Alas, the Mexican vacation ended and both went their separate ways, Ruth back to New York and Harter to Des Moines, his home base. The thing was, Harter Hull would often take business trips, and New York City was still the center of the known universe. Surely he could make his way back there whenever he wished and apparently he wished to an awful, awful lot over the next few months, sometimes on business, and sometimes for Ruth. Every visit together was like a romantic escape to Paris, always some lavish shopping, fancy restaurants, and romantic evenings. This then would not be a simple vacation fling, but a full-fledged affair, as Harter while separated, was still a married man. His affliction to alcohol had also played a role in both his choices, as well as his separation from Peggy at that point.

Once more, nature exacted its revenge and Ruth got pregnant. She had already had Stephen a couple years prior, whom she had partially given up for adoption to Agnes, and had aborted once before as well. This was illegitimate pregnancy number three, as far anyone knew.

The thing was, for as much as Ruth was infatuated with Harter, their time together was sporadic. Thus, Ruth continued to occasionally entertain other male suitors. In truth, Ruth was not completely sure who the father of this child was, as she was also courted frequently during that same timeframe by an executive from the New York Telephone company. This, perhaps, drove the decision-making that was to follow.

Ruth had fallen in love with Harter and she felt he had fallen in love with her, there was an undeniable attraction. The problem was, whereas Ruth had never married, Harter had Peggy back in Des Moines. He also had two children of his own already with Peggy – the first son, my half brother, and only daughter, Ginger. He was considered somewhat of a bastion of his community and a high-profile husband and family man.

Women like Ruth have been in this situation many times over the course of history. There are numerous ways to play out the situation, none of them very original. Ruth wanted, more than anything, for Harter to cleave to her, to choose her over Peggy in Iowa, but not out of parental obligation for this reproductive accident, which might not have even been his, but because he truly was in love with her and wanted her more than his current wife.

She put it to Harter directly: "Where is this relationship going? I want you. I do not want to share you with Peggy. Are you going to leave her for me or not?" At no time did she say a single word about her pregnancy however. She did not want that to factor into his decision-making.

The gambit failed. Harter professed his love but was torn, not wanting to break up his family and his well-earned reputation as an upstanding and true family man in Des Moines. He indicated Peggy would never leave him, and his kids my half brother and Ginger were too important and too young for him to consider leaving her. He was torn.

Ruth told him to leave and never see her again as a result. It was a self-destructive decision, but a decision nonetheless. She did not ask him for money or any other form of support for her dilemma, again fearing that by doing so she would push his hand towards decisions that were not fully in his heart. By now Ruth Wilband was 39-years-old. Most women would have used the accidental pregnancy to entrap their man one way or the other. But this was not Ruth's way. Harter went away, unaware of her pregnancy.

Once more, for whatever reason, Ruth decided to have the baby rather than abort. Perhaps it was the still-existing illegality of the procedure, although there was always Mexico or some other country. Perhaps it was Catholic guilt. Nonetheless, she again decided to carry the baby to term.

Perhaps had this happened today, Ruth at 39 might have thought more seriously about keeping this baby and raising it on her own, but in the early 1960's this was not the norm by any means. Instead, she continued to live and work in New York – Brooklyn to be exact – for about four or five months more until she started to show. From there she returned once more to the welcoming arms of Saint John in Canada. Again, many women of this era might have thought twice, for certainly Saint John meant family and those who had known her for years, whereas New York meant blending in with throngs of faceless, unopinionated millions. But Saint John was home, and home has many meanings, meanings far beyond merely where one hangs one's hat. Home is where they understand you; it is where people love you unconditionally, no matter how badly you screw up.

Agnes took her in. This, of course, meant sharing all the details of the scandal with her, but Agnes placed family above judgementalism and welcomed her warmly into her home, and kept her secret from others. There, Ruth got to also share time with her first child, Stephen, who was well aware through the years of exactly who Ruth was and who she was to him. It was an odd family situation, but an honest one, insofar as Stephen was concerned.

What would she do with this new child however? Many options were considered, but in the end the decision was made to go through Catholic Charities and place the child up for adoption. The Wilbands had faith in the organization and the process and felt a good family would be found, most likely one that lived nearby.

The concept of putting a child up for adoption yet holding on somehow through correspondence with the adoptive parents was quite frowned upon back in this era. It was always thought best to make a clean break and allow the new family to bond without fear of interlopers coming into the child's life and confusing it. This must have pained Ruth somewhat, compared to how she still had a relationship with Stephen, but at the end of the day, traditional adoption was the way she decided to go.

Regarding all of this, Harter Hull was completely in the dark. He had no idea a woman was possibly carrying a baby of his, nor did he have any say in how the matter was handled. He was totally and completely oblivious. He had gone back to Peggy, gone back to Iowa, and it would appear he and Ruth Wilband were nothing more than history to one another. Ruth, for her part, thought more and more that the baby was the progeny of another man, perhaps the executive with the telephone company, and married as well, the man Ruth was seeing in-between Harter's visits. Either way, neither man knew of any of this.

After placing the child, a boy, up for adoption in her hometown, Ruth recuperated with Agnes in Saint John a short while before returning to Brooklyn. As time went by, Harter Hull became as distant a memory as this child she had placed up for adoption. Other men came into her life and existence, for Ruth, went on as it had before Harter. Her social calendar remained booked, despite her burgeoning age. Ruth was still a looker and a social gadfly, dancing and carousing wherever there was fun to be had.

A few years later, nature struck again for the fourth time. Ruth became pregnant with another child by another man. Once more, this man was not a man she had any designs on marrying. Only Harter Hull had ever fit that description in her life. In fact, the father of the unborn child was the husband of a friend of Ruth and Joan's, another product of an extramarital affair with a straying husband. And so, it was without anywhere near as much thought that Ruth, now on her own again, decided what to do about this unwanted pregnancy.

The well-worn path between New York and Saint John was again trod. Agnes, stalwart Agnes, once more came to the rescue. Again, Ruth wanted to go through with the pregnancy and bring this baby to term. Unlike Harter Hull's baby, though, or whoever's baby the last one was, there now appeared another branch of the Wilband family who was desirous of a child in their lives. Ruth's brother Eddie and his wife asked if they might rear the child and Ruth consented, seeing as how successful the situation with Sister Agnes raising Stephen had worked out. Eddie and his wife lived in Ontario. And so another son, this one named Blake, was born and given to Eddie to raise as his and his wife's own. Once more, Ruth Wilband, childless and single, returned once again to New York City.

For all the similarities, there were differences in the upbringing of Stephen versus the upbringing of Blake. Stephen always knew who he was, as in he knew that Ruth was his mother, yet Agnes was the mother who would adopt and raise him. On the other hand, Stephen did not know about the other children in his biological mother's life. He did not know of the baby put up by Ruth for adoption nor did he know of the genesis of Blake, his half brother. Frankly, he did not know that Blake *was* his half brother. This all stemmed from *Blake* not being told that Ruth was his biological mother.

Why was all this done in such a fashion? No nefarious reason. It simply was that each mother – who does the actual raising of a child – makes her own personal decision as to how to raise that child insofar as explaining origins. Agnes wanted Stephen to know who he was and how he came about and so it would be. Blake's mother – Eddie's wife – chose a different route. Who was right and who was wrong is nothing more than a personal opinion. Each woman did what she thought best and did it with love and caring, as they personally saw it. And so while each boy grew up knowing of the other, treating the other as a cousin, neither knew they were, in actuality, half brothers. And neither knew anything about the third boy – the one who had been put up for adoption to strangers, somewhere in New Brunswick most likely. Blake eventually found out that he was adopted, and so he assumed that he and Stephen were cousins but not by blood, although their blood connection was far closer than had ever been imagined.

Following a 2 year separation and ultimate divorce from Peggy, Harter remarried for 5 years to Marge. He failed at this marriage also, and again alcohol assisted the process. The 1960s slowly became the 1970s and something changed in Harter Hull's life. A woman he had not seen nor heard of for years nagged at his consciousness. It drove him further and further from his wife Peggy, so far that he began obsessing about Ruth and making plans for reversing the decision he had made years early when Ruth had asked him to choose between her and Peggy and he had chosen his wife and family in Iowa. With his kids a bit older now, albeit not old enough yet perhaps, Harter Hull wanted a redo.

Harter, the traveling man, made another trek back to New York, but Ruth no longer resided where she once had in Brooklyn. He could not find her name in any New York City telephone book. Short of hiring a private detective, he instead recalled hearing her speak of Canada and Saint John, recollecting her telling tales of her family there and referring to them by name for him.

Harter flew up to New Brunswick and landed unannounced on the doorstep of Ruth's sister Agnes, explaining to her his tale of a broken heart. Agnes first slammed the door in his face. Agnes may have thought this was the end of the adventure, but Harter the "sales king" was not to be trifled with. He remained in Saint John and came back to her house the very next day, pleading ever more so for information as to Ruth's whereabouts. Again, Agnes refused his entrees. This went on and on for days until finally Agnes realized this was something other than an old paramour looking to rekindle a one-night stand. His persistence paid off and Agnes finally relented by telling Harter where to find her.

At that moment, Ruth was living with another man in New York, which would explain why a phone under her own name no longer could be found by directory assistance.

Harter flew down to New York, looked up Ruth at the address of this other man, and then set about doing the same to her as he had to Agnes – confronting her on her doorstep and refusing to go away and stay away until she would agree to hear him out. Harter was a salesman and indeed, this would be his most impassioned sales job.

Like with Agnes, Harter with his relentless DNA of never backing off a passion or cause, wore Ruth down. He pulled out his signature charm, as she heard him out and agreed to begin seeing him again. As she closed her eyes to contemplate this decision, he would gently kiss her closed eye lids and state that he could not take his eyes off of her, that she always felt like a warm fitting sweater when they were together. As per her previous request of him, she asked that she be his number one, that he leave Peggy. This time, unlike the last, he did. Harter divorced Marg, and then convinced Ruth to accompany him back to Des Moines, Iowa to be his new wife.

It was stressful and it was scandalous, but the heart wants what the heart wants. Ruth Wilband finally became Mrs. Harter B. Hull II in June 9, 1973, at the age of 47, a married woman after all these years. On September 3, 1974, Ruth also became a naturalized American citizen for the first time.

It must have felt odd at times, Harter and Ruth living in the same city as his first wife, Peggy, and their children, but Harter was established there and he wanted to remain close to his two children. The strain of a new marriage that broke apart a family however, this proved difficult. Ruth attempted to fit into the Des Moines social scene on Harter's arm, but for so many years, he had been known as Peggy's husband. Who was this new woman, anyway; this New Yorker, this Canadian? This was made even harder on them both, as Harter swiftly moved Ruth out to Des Moines with him almost a year prior to their official wedding ceremony. He could not leave Des Moines on any permanent basis due to his business concerns, and he did not want to have a long-distance relationship with Ruth once more for fear she might meet another. And so they spent their first year together in Des Moines "living in sin," prior to making their relationship official.

Unfortunately, the new marriage of true love and romance did not last long. Harter tragically died early into their new lives together, following a 3 day struggle in the hospital, after a heart failure while eating dinner one evening in 1975. And sadly, poor Peggy, with Harter being her first and only love, was not even informed of his passing. His last few years he lived hard, almost daring death to take him. A very sad footnote, especially to his first wife Peggy and the kids, was that Ruth had not contacted them to inform them of Harter's passing. Peggy's mother actually found out from a mutual acquaintance. Very sad way to hear about the death of a family member.

Prior to his passing, Harter had gotten more and more nostalgic for the war, going back to Europe at least once a year to see the cities where he was stationed and even the cities he bombed. During these trips he would religiously visit the since abandoned airstrip where his 487th bomb group from the US 8th AF flew out from, Levenham, England. He would take the long trip to the UK, drive out to the abandoned Lavenham 8th AF airstrip, and then get out of the car by himself usually saying nothing at all to Ruth about the ritual each time, walk from one end of the run down airplane runway to the other as Ruth waited for him in the car, then walk back to the car and sit for a moment staring out the runway. There were not tears, but clearly there was pain within his eyes as he looked steely outward in a somewhat lost stare. Then, without words to Ruthy, he would put the car in drive and leave within the hour. A day to get there, a short walk, some reflection of thoughts unknown, then off. It was a strange ritual, but one he seemed to feel he had to make, as if he was reconnecting with something or making a karmic atonement of some sort. The departure each mission starting off with such pride to accomplish their task, contrasted quickly with anxiety surrounding the worry of making it back safely perhaps lingered during each walk. The few occasions when their B17 received either a direct or flack hit, resulting in a belly-turret gunner not making it back with the fellow crew members, could also be possibly remembered in silent honor and a short prayer. The shear relief that would come with the chirping sound of the tires touching down on the runway signaling all would be ok for another day - perhaps another reason to be thankful for being able to walk and touch this ground again. He would never officially explain himself, so one can only conjecture. But a part of him seemed left on the battlefields of Europe and always would be.

In the end, as a result of the many scars the war left on him, he drank a lot – scotch was his fancy – and was a heavy smoker. Lucky Strike was his brand, or as Ginger once referred to them – 'his unlikely strikes'. He knew both were bad for him, particularly to the extreme extent he indulged during his later years, but he seemed not to care, or more likely felt invincible based on his persona.

Tragedy would also befall Blake, Ruth's son who was raised by Eddie. Blake developed what was possibly alopecia, a disease that causes loss of all body hair as well as the hair on the head. It is an autoimmune disorder that is rarely completely treatable, although Blake's doctors did attempt some experimental treatments and medications.

Details of Blake's challenges being unclear, what was clear is that there were sound-bites shared of fragmented elements, none of which were completely verified however. Alopecia was not Blake's only problem, as he became increasingly unhappy and moody, often opting for self-destructive behavior. Blake's situation, which became apparent in his late teens to early twenties, was possibly exacerbated by his discovering the truth about his adoption. How exactly this came about is a matter of conjecture, but come out it did and Blake was none too happy about his having lived his life as someone else's secret. Blake came to know that his birth mother was his "Aunt Ruth." The issue upset him greatly and he felt betrayed and lied to.

Blake also had another stressful dilemma in his life at this time: he had a girlfriend whom he had recently broke up with. Rumors of a possible pregnancy did not help his stress levels. Between all of these burdens, poor Blake was breaking down physically as well as emotionally.

Blake was on a particular medication regimen, for both his alopecia as well as his stress, where he had been told by his doctor not to imbibe alcohol. The problem is, this sort of warning is so common, even with innocuous over-the-counter medications, that many patients simply nod their heads and then go off and ignore the plea. Were that Blake had taken this particular warning more seriously. A friend of his was getting married and weddings tend to be big social events, particularly with bachelor parties and the like. To swear off alcohol completely when one is actively involved in a buddy's wedding is almost cruel.

Blake succumbed. After only a couple drinks, Blake took on all the manifestations of a man drunk to the gills due to the medication. He was found stumbling and bumbling around the streets of town, looking to the world like a man greatly in need of a night to sleep it off. The local police came upon him and took him into custody for that very reason, cuffing him and then escorting him into the local drunk tank.

There was no torture or any other form of seriously inappropriate behavior on the side of the police. In actuality, they simply ignored Blake as they tended to ignore most inebriated cellmates. They were thus unable to discern Blake's sudden turn for the worse, as his sleep turned into coma, his brain being affected severely from the combination of prescription drugs and alcohol. When they attempted to stir him, he was already dead. He had not yet reached his 23rd birthday.

As to the child she had prior to Blake, Ruth never told Harter that he had a son. Why? More than anything else, at that time she was never completely sure the baby she put up for adoption was his. To have worried and concerned him so over an issue of confusing and undetermined detail would have been, in her opinion, unnecessary. Furthermore, Harter was a man of action, a take-control, own-the-room kind of man, larger than life. If he thought for a moment such a child existed and it might be his, he would have moved heaven and earth to find this child and get to the bottom of the situation. Ruth knew this about him and it most certainly must have factored into her thinking on the matter. Thus, Harter Hull died having no idea he might have had a third child somewhere in the world, a half-brother to both Ginger and my half brother, a child with his loving Ruth.

Ruth's marriage to Harter may have been short, but for her, it was most certainly luxurious. Harter did not, though, come into all of the Hull fortune amassed by his own father, as his mother, who existed into her nineties, outlived him and thus was the primarily beneficiary of Harter's father's money, although Harter also had a sister who also outlived him. In the end, what was left of the estate of Harter's father seemed to go almost exclusively from his mother down to his sister. Still, what money Harter and Ruth had was more than Ruth had ever before accrued. Things were good.

When Harter died, Ruth was his primary beneficiary. The child he had with Ruth years prior, of course, particularly since its paternity had never been determined and had been put up for adoption to a pair of strangers, never factored into any of this. Ruth had only seldom put thought to the child she put up for adoption, as in her mind he was with a caring family, safe and happy. The birthday of the young one often made her think of him however, what might he look like, how is his life evolving, or the like.

And so Ruth, alone and single once more, now with money, but not only that, she then had a stake in a company – the insurance company Harter had started. The thing was, Harter had taken on partners toward the end of his days. Ruth knew absolutely nothing of the insurance business. She, in fact, had no knowledge of how to run any business of any significant size, nor did she have any desire to suddenly become a business mogul so late into her own life.

Before, as a single woman, Ruth had to live hand to mouth, but like Blanche DuBois in "A Streetcar Named Desire", she had also always "relied on the kindness of strangers," in her case "strangers" being dashing young men, most of them somewhat or rather wealthy. She frequently overspent in those days, too, but somehow or other, some man would come along and bail her out of her present dilemma. But now she had significant amounts of cash money in hand, a situation that was completely new to her. There would be no creditors knocking at the door. What she had not figured out, though, was that this money was finite. She gave no concern to Harter's business; only to the money that now bulged her bank account. There was also no budgeting. There was no thought of tomorrow. All in all, it was all pretty immature, although not in any way malicious. Ruth spent on herself, but she also spent generously on others. Her sisters and brothers, as well as their children now were able to look forward to being lavished with presents from "rich Aunt Ruth." Spending delighted her.

As for Harter's partners, it became readily apparent that Ruth Wilband Hull would be nothing more than a financial liability to them and would bring nothing else positive to the table. A silent partner may have been one thing, but a silent partner who quite obviously could not manage her own household finances could become quite a problem. They most likely feared Ruth blowing through Harter's bank accounts and then coming in demanding more, more, more, far more than would be in the company's best interests since again, Harter himself was no longer on the scene to make a positive contribution to the company via his mind and his efforts. Ruth, to them, was nothing more than a leaky hole in their corporate bucket. She was also a person devoid of the wisdom to seek advice. Had she sought proper counsel, Ruth could have lived in luxury for all of the rest of her days. Instead, she came when called by Harter's partners, and did as they told her. She signed papers; it seemed they were always having her sign papers. She knew not what she was signing, for she trusted them. They seemed like such nice fellows. It was only long after papers were signed and out of her hands that she was informed she had given away ownership interest in the company to Harter's partners. Whatever money she now had, that was all she wrote. There would be no more. Still, she seemed unconcerned. She had been paid and she had money in the bank. What did she care about some boring old insurance company? She wasn't going to sit glassy-eyed through corporate board meetings. These nice men were going to take that off of her plate. They would be the ones with all that responsibility. Ruth just got a check and a warm handshake. Life was good and would only get better.

Things changed almost overnight at Brokers Clearing House. They changed their legal entity and their corporate image and eventually spun to the world that they only began operations at that point in 1975. To hear them tell it now, the company only began once Harter B. Hull died. His official, public corporate legacy is that he never lived and never founded a company, a company that made him a very comfortable man. How sad.

As years went on, Ruth continued her spending ways. Not a cent of what she had was ever invested, even though it was readily apparent that there was no source of new income. It was almost childlike, tragically enough. Ruth was no longer a young woman, but was certainly not yet old enough that the money she had would last, at least at the rate at which it was being spent. But this was not the sort of thing Ruth sat down and tried to figure out.

Through all of this, Ruth remained in Des Moines, her new hometown. She was untethered and could have just as easily moved back to New York or Saint John, but she had managed, over a scant few years, to establish herself as the new Mrs. Harter Hull and she liked it. Never before had she had station in life and now, here in Iowa, she did. She missed Harter, missed him terribly, but her life had changed so very much and Des Moines was now a part of all that.

Ruth remained single for a few years, but then eventually began dating again. She finally met a fellow by the name of Bill Lyman and they married; Ruth's second marriage. He was not as wealthy as Harter, but together they seemed comfortable. Comfortable and happy.

CHAPTER FOUR

A DIAMOND IN THE ROUGH

"Education is a progressive discovery of our own ignorance."

Will Durant

To me the word 'education' has only little to do with formal schooling. I've always been intrigued with talking to older people who've 'been around'. During my bartending and doorman days in PEI, throughout day shifts on the weekends I'd have the pleasure of talking to many 'seasoned' individuals who would share with me a little of their lives over a drink or two. The benefit of being on the other side of the bar, is that the meaning of their words would take deeper roots, and become more a part of the fabric of your being, helping to form your own views on life.

I recall once during a Saturday afternoon working at a bar call Gentleman Jims, when I served at a small table a lone 60-something looking man. He looked very proper, smart suit, grayed hair, and carried himself with a certain distinction. I could tell from his demeanor however, after serving him his second drink, that he was quite 'distant' and a bit lost in his gaze. Since it wasn't busy I decided to sit down and say hello, and ask him how his day was going. He seemed surprised I was asking, and looked at me and said, 'he was about your age, my son'. Not picking up on the inference I replied 'Does he go to the University?' He answered in a very factual, yet sad tone as he said 'He died in a car accident on Friday, and yes, he went to Holland College'. I was immediately choked up a bit, so I had to of gather myself as I mustered a few questions to keep the conversation afloat. While serving others in parallel, I came back his table several times out of pure curiosity to understand how he was handling the gravity of what had happened to him and his family. We had what was for me, one of my first 'adult' conversations, where I truly was interested in absolutely everything he had to say. He told me on his son's aspirations, his personality, and of his own desires for his son. I could read the pain in his face in every shift of his eyebrows as he told his story, and I sensed it in every wrinkle on his forehead as he expressed both his pride and sorrow. This created an inflection point for me, to be able to actually listen to more than just words as others shared elements of their personal lives. The conversation itself, plus the entire experience created in me from that moment on a unique desire to seek out opportunities to talk to people of experience, as I became aware then the value of sharing such experiences.

I received my first degree from the University of Prince Edward Island and then went on to get a second degree from the University of New Brunswick in Fredericton. During my stint at UNB, I took what they call a "professional experience year." In my case it meant taking a job with IBM. I loved it. It's one thing to sit in a classroom and still another to roll up your sleeves and get into the labs on campus. But working in the real world is on a whole other level. I don't see how anyone can come out of college with any value to their future employer, at least in the field of engineering and management, without some of that practical experience under their belt.

The IBM internship was very competitive. They only took five interns from Canada that year, from the various engineering disciplines, to come to Toronto to work. I recall in the selection interview process with IBM executives, one senior hiring executive 'Mr. Cohen' asking me why I wanted this job. Cohen was the epitome of a professional executive, and highly respected in the organization. I certainly had no experience in job interviews, so wasn't prepared for the question, but I looked directly at him and said, "Mr. Cohen, I don't want to get your coffee. I don't want to photocopy your documents. I want to work. I want to learn and show you what I can do with that learning". I'm not exactly sure, but that could have been the single smartest thing I said in that multi hour interview. I was over the moon with the thrill and excitement of being selected. I mean, come on; IBM? That was the big leagues back then; there was no better job and for no better money, especially for a no name kid from the northern part of Saint John.

It was a 15-month stint – full school year flanked by both summers, and it was quite the win/win. IBM got cheap engineering grunt work, and we got real life experience and "IBM" on our resumes. Granted, they worked us like dogs. Honestly, we would have done anything for them, anything at all; we felt so lucky to be there. Of course, once the fifteen months were over it was back to university, back to acting like a student again. It was an odd feeling, as if we'd had that first taste of reality and now we were being treated like kiddies again. But we adapted; we had to.

The other great thing about such a program is if you did well and didn't burn your bridges, you were likely to get a job offer from the firm with which you did your internship. I was lucky to have been well-liked and IBM had a job waiting for me for when I graduated. That was the way to do it and take full advantage of the opportunity provided, and enter into your final year of school stress free, job in hand.

The only problem, if there was one, was that the opportunity with IBM was in the big city of Toronto, where I also did my internship. I mean, for me there was no problem at all, I had just spent a year there. What young man with a college degree and a great job waiting for him wouldn't want to be single, have dollars in his pocket, and living in some very large metropolitan city? But that was me. On the other side of the equation was my poor mother, who was worried to tears, her youngest heading to the big smoke of T-O. I was finally leaving the nest for good, leaving Saint John and the old neighborhood, with no real reason to return except to visit on holidays and such. Mom was somewhat inconsolable. She cared so much for Marcel and me that she worried about everything related to us, all the time. Our home was very typical. A mother yelling at the boys to pick up, behave, do homework etc., but also so full of love, and not just from my mother, but from my father as well. I could never have asked for a better family, really. But now it was time to make my own way into the big, bad world.

At IBM I was doing process engineering, designing and developing new manufacturing processes, particularly in the 'new at the time' technology of surface mount technology (SMT) robotics. I loved it. Down the road, the division I was working in would eventually split off manufacturing Operations from IBM due to our excess capacity and form an entirely new company by the name of Celestica, which is still around today. Needless to say, it was vital work. I guess there are a lot of people in the world, even in engineering, who feel all they do is move piles of paper from one stack to another, not really being creative or causing any positive change in the world or in the marketplace, but where I was working, we felt we were really on the cutting edge and it was heady stuff, especially for a young guy like me fresh out of university. Every day was a new learning experience, hands on, doing my thing. The mentorships were plenty, starting with Brian Derdall, a sort of rain-man genius in Engineering, along with T-man the technology guru, new hire peers Alex and Joel, and my new senior co-workers Ivan, Robert, and a sort of management mentor John. John played a big role in helping me find my way at Big-Blue, and was also a good friend.

We were doing roughly $2+ billion dollars worth of manufacturing right there at that site, which gives you a kind of clue of how important and how big an operation it was. Often unknown to those south of the border, Canadian technology companies are extremely competitive, and we were incredibly important to the IBM empire at that time, and IBM knew it and appreciated it. As the marketplace shifted, we at IBM had excess capacity – yet unlike many of our peers IBM locations around the world, we were still profitable in Toronto, so we had the ability to take on an even bigger load, which also made us all feel we were in the right place at the right time. No downsizing or outsourcing for us. This would prove a bit ironic later.

As time passed and business evolved, we ended up becoming a wholly owned subsidiary of IBM, giving ourselves a new name, which helped us take on contracts that might not otherwise have wanted to work directly with IBM, companies such as Apple, for instance, their arch rival who needed capable outsourcing partners.

After a year or so at IBM/Celestica, I got solicited to get into the networking world – telecommunications, another hot, hot field. A company in Ottawa by the name of Newbridge Networks, later to be purchased by Alcatel, asked me to come and join them. I was recruited by what could best be described as a mad-man maverick in the company at the time, a loyal soldier to the company's founder Terrance Mathews, named Dave Gordon. He recruited me hard, as they were growing fast, and needed some of the specific experience I had gained at IBM. Newbridge was super big in telecommunications, providing products and services for all of the who's who in the game: AT&T, Bridge Telecom, Bell Canada, you name it. It was a publically traded company. When I joined, they were just under a billion in annual revenue. I came over as a Director of Strategic Relationships in Operations, and worked there four years or so initially. Eventually I became Vice President of Manufacturing and General Manager at the site – but this was after first taking a stint at another company. Ironically it was mad-man Dave again who recruited me back to Newbridge a couple years later.

The company grew very fast. I stayed for a while and would have stayed longer, but I was approached again, this time by a company called JDS Fitel, which would later be known in Canada as JDS Uniphase following a large merger. I went to JDS as a Director of Strategy & Integration for the newly formed mergers and acquisitions group. Cutting through the jargon, the group had to make the decisions as to what we would try to develop in-house and what we would purchase outside of the company, often in the form of actually buying some other company that was already in existence and was making a product we felt we had to have. Once decisions were made on what technologies were to be pursued and acquired, my job was to work with the acquired company to work the transitional elements of bringing that business into the mothership, integrate into our various divisions the pieces to keep – and cut the balance for the financial synergies to be realized.

Fiber optic technologies were taking off like mad and we were in the thick of it. We were on the passive component side, meaning no lasers or transmitters; it was all things you could pass light through and affect the light in some way, such as splitting it or combining it or amplifying it. One of the mergers we eventually did was with a company named Uniphase. It was, at the time, one of the largest mergers in Canadian history. Uniphase, as a separate entity, was the largest *active* optical component company, meaning they were the guys who *were* making the lasers for transmitting light. We merged with them for $6.1 billion dollars on Jan 29, 1999. That merger, along with other responsibilities, pretty much kept me very busy for about a year.

After we finished that, the company was growing so fast that the then Senior VP of operations asked my current VP of Strategy boss if I could come over to their side and temporarily help them in Ops, as they were having challenges in ramping a specific mechanical-optical switch product. I had obviously been involved in manufacturing operations before, so it was a good fit for me. I finished a current assignment quickly, then started to come in for some Ops meetings and spent a lot of time with the VP under him to see if this would work out for all parties concerned. I was led to believe it was a temporary assignment where I would help them out for four to six months before going back to my old duties.

Two weeks later, this VP asked me to his staff meeting, which was kind of odd for me, since I was simply helping out the VP underneath him. When I showed up, the guy I'd been working with was not there. The Senior VP didn't bat an eye; he just began introducing me to the senior staff while telling them I'd be helping them in that particular department for a while. He then politely asked if he could have a word with me outside in the hall. Once there, he pointed down the hall and said, "Go down there to so-and-so's office (the manufacturing VP I'd been interfacing with to help). Why don't you go down there and get briefed on what's going on? Once you're done, come on back and join us." It sounded innocent enough, although a bit strange.

I walked down the hall and into the office to which I'd been directed. There was the fellow I thought I'd be working with. I knew him well as we worked at Newbridge together prior – it's a small world in most every industry once you've been around a while – and I liked and respected him. But what I saw said more than words. There were his belongings in a cardboard box – his pictures, his trophies, his pens and his paperclips. The box was wedged against the door, holding it open as he packed. He looked at me forlornly as he wiped the place clean of anything that was his. "You are fucking kidding me," I said, and he replied, "No, it's exactly what it looks like. Good luck in your new job." He'd been fired and I guess I was to assume some of his duties. I was not his assistant, his helper, his comrade, or his wingman. I was his replacement and he was suddenly out of a job, something neither of us knew anything about until only a few moments ago in his case, and that very minute in mine. Business is cruel like that sometimes. Watching him, I knew someday the roles would be reversed and some other guy would have to stand sentry as I cleared out my belongings. It's a humbling experience.

I went back to the staff meeting in progress somewhat in a haze. I believe the big boss said some nice things about me; I really can't say for sure. I was too stunned. I was happy for the vote of confidence to pick up more responsibility, but I felt very uncomfortable about how things were handled. It's like in war when you see your first dead body. You know it's a part of the job, but it still messes with you when you see it for the first time close up. I mean, I'd seen screw-ups fired before; that's a part of life. But you always think that if you do good work, you're safe. Well, no, in this world, you're not, although it's still better to be good and work hard than to not.

I got back to the staff meeting and sat down, wondering what the Senior VP had told the rest of the staff. At some point the fog was lifted when I heard the boss say, "And now Mike has something he would like to tell us." Huh? That sort of thing will get you to snap to right quick. Heck, I'd already seen my fate were I to not be prepared for whatever they threw at me – as he and I actually never even discussed what had just happened or the implication to my job. I got to my feet and blathered on about something or other. I briefly said, "It is unfortunately that so-and-so's last day is today, and I'll be picking up some of his responsibilities – but I'll need your help for sure." I must have made it sound good because they kept me on. I worked to improve issues in the areas needing most work, and I felt I did good work there, work I was proud of.

When I left my predecessor's office earlier that day, after seeing his box packed, I'd said that I would buy him a beer after work to understand better what just happened, and he took me up on it. I wanted there to be no hard feelings and there weren't. He knew the score and would eventually land on his feet. Heck, some day I may find myself working for him!

The whole way this fellow's firing was handled stuck with me, though. They talk a lot in this world about corporate culture, and for as much as I respected what this company was doing in the marketplace, I didn't like how some things were being done personnel-wise. My old employers at Newbridge must have been reading my mind at that time, because my phone rang and there was Dave, asking me back with a much higher salary and position. Of course Dave was smart about not letting me think too much about the new offer to come back, so he invited me out to a small Italian restaurant-bar with offer in hand. He was smart, as after a couple bottles of Amarone, I signed the papers. I had always liked Newbridge, so I decided to leave the bad feelings of what had happened to my colleague behind and grabbed it and went along for the ride. I knew a lot of the people still back there; I'd even hired a number of them myself from when I previously worked there. They were giving me a large team to head, which is a lot of responsibility, and with responsibility comes reward. When things like that happen, going back to a former employer, it's not a backwards move, even though it's a place you've been before. It's a tip of the hat to the work you'd done there and it was definitely not a lateral move. I was moving up and up again and it felt good. Dave is now retired and is writing and recording music, his first passion from days prior to the high-tech world, and we remain good friends.

Newbridge had a longer term plan to get itself purchased by a larger

company. To the uninitiated this may sound like defeat and retreat but in the business world, it's anything but. Part of my job was to clean up things on the Operations side and make us look as attractive as possible to a potential buyer and then to help in selling to that buyer. It's sort of like giving someone a makeover, or being a realtor and "staging" a house to attract a buyer at a high price. It takes skill to "paint the house for a sale;" it's not just window dressing, but removing a lot of excess costs and overhead associated with organizational structure. Working closely with a consulting firm, we did what was needed to prepare both the organization as well as the due diligence documentation for potential buyers.

There were a couple of different suitors. In the end, Alcatel, a large French company, came in, liked what they saw, and picked us up for over $7 billion dollars; a very good deal for us. They kept me on, making me VP and general manager of Canadian operations. I stayed on board for a year or so. Part of the deal was that if I stayed on at least a year I'd get a nice salary bonus and I liked the sound of that – who wouldn't?

After that, I really wasn't looking to get out, but it was clear that most decisions were being made at corporate head quarters in France and although I was a good soldier and did what was decided, I was not always consulted like I had been before. I was then approached by some guys who had come from Nortel, a big company at the time, who were itching to go out and do their own thing and were looking for some additional talent to round out their team. James, the bright charismatic COO, and Peter the seasoned exec CEO, were building a team of experienced management and engineers to take on what was a huge effort for a new company. A start-up is always a risk, but once you've been in the business world a while, you come to learn that start-ups are something you always have to do at least once in your life. It's almost a rite of passage. Here I'd been, working for all these established companies all this time. I'd never really flown by the seat of my pants, the way you would with a start-up, wondering if you'd even reach the point where you'd have desks and stationary, let alone a salary. Daredevil stuff, but incredibly lucrative if you scored. I mean, who wouldn't want to have been part of Bill Gates' first team at Microsoft?

Again, they cast me as VP of Ops. They had already gotten started with the company on the R&D side, and now needed to add the operational team. The company initially raised something like $188 million dollars, a huge amount. This was one of the largest war chests for a startup in Canada at the time, and this was only the first round. My first task was not just to build a manufacturing team, but first to find us a building, as I couldn't even build a team yet until we had a place to put them. When hiring began in earnest, I put about 100 operations people on the payroll. We had another 200 or so in research and development as well as general and administrative. Our purpose for being was to deal with a common problem in telecommunications at the time, which was a bottleneck in communication data flow from city to city. We used something known as DWDM, or Dense Wavelength Division Multiplexing. It involves putting different data sources together on optical fiber with each signal carried at the same time on its own separate light wavelength. It's even more complicated than that, but suffice it to say it became the state of the art in telecommunications because it worked. Networking had always had massive amounts of inefficiencies – and in this case this company, Innovance Networks, targeted some of those for removal. The company felt there was a crying need for solutions in order to streamline wireless as well as hard-wired communications.

Innovance created a whole different way of managing optical-to-electrical bottlenecks at the core switching points in the network, and set out to create a truly "transparent" optical network –optical switches at the core instead of multiple costly conversions from optical to electrical and back. It sounded like an impossible task, but we had some incredibly strong minds, plucked from Nortel and other places. Ambitious young guys and gals who wanted the freedom to create the next generation of communications. It didn't happen overnight, of course. It took about three years for us to show much for our efforts.

There were also problems with the marketplace. We came to discover that business analysts were often full of crap, but what they said had an incredible affect on the marketplace. The prognosticators kept saying there was greater and greater need for capacity, which we kept saying was untrue. But the people in the industry were also financing the customers they sold to and they thus had a heavy motivation to keep driving sales by telling people they needed more, more, more, even if they truly didn't. In the end, everyone overbuilt their networks. Here we were, a new company that has built a better mousetrap, but our potential customer base was already overburdened financially with all they had already invested into technology they truly did not need. It was a real problem.

We had approximately 350 employees, the best and brightest in the business. The entry-level engineers were all making over six figures, so you can imagine the kind of money it took to keep the upper level superstars happy. But the realities, idiotic as they were looking back, beat us up in the marketplace. Our burn-rate was very high, and we eventually simply ran out of money. Pretty soon we were laying people off and laying people off. Me, I was safe because I was one of a handful of executives left to wind down operations. I and a few others would be the ones to turn off the lights as the last ones out, if need be.

We knew our ideas were strong. We tried to sell ourselves off to another company, but nobody was buying at the time because of the same market madness that had hurt us in the first place. In the end, we had to shut the doors and yes, I was the last one out of the very building I found three years prior. My first start-up, and I was there from its cradle to its grave. This was not quite the lucrative exit strategy we envisioned at the onset of the company.

I liked those guys, but it was every man for himself. We all went our separate ways, grabbing the best positions where we could. Most of us went to the highest bidder, which was often some large, established firm. As for me, I did the crazy thing of casting my lot in with another start-up by the name of BreconRidge, out of Ottawa. It was to be a contract manufacturing concern and it featured a lot of players from the same companies I'd already been interfacing with over the years. Seems most of the larger telecommunications companies dropped manufacturing in favor of outsourcing, so a niche suddenly developed. I came in and was named VP of Global Manufacturing.

Of course, to read this, it would appear that all life was to me was work, work, and more work. And yes, while the work was exciting and the opportunities wonderful and lucrative, man cannot live on work alone. My immediate post-University years leading up to this high-tech rollercoaster were certainly filled with plenty of adventure and life learning as well.

Right after I graduated from my first university, I fell in love, and no, not just with some job, but with a woman, a beautiful girl named Kira. She was on vacation from Montreal in Prince Edward Island, where I was working that summer at a local beachside roadhouse called Thirsty's. One of her brothers was in the military and living out around Prince Edward Island at the time and invited her out to visit him. When we met, it was instant sparks and we knew we were a match.

Kira followed me to the University of New Brunswick and enrolled there as well. When I got my job at IBM, she followed me to Toronto. She took classes there as well, while I worked. We were a couple, plain and simple. We did everything together and we appeared headed for marriage, no doubt about it. All of our plans involved one another. Neither of us made a decision about our futures without bouncing it off of the other.

Kira was, as I said, absolutely beautiful. What was she doing with me, I sometimes wondered in jest? She had curly blond hair, full lips, and a big smile for everyone; like a young Julia Roberts looking type. She didn't tell me until we'd been dating nearly two months that she had actually been modeling in Montreal. She'd even done some acting, appearing in a television commercial for Guess Jeans.

She was pretty modest. I was once walking through a mall with a few of my guy pals when we passed through the lady's bathing suit store.

There was a poster on the wall and matching tags hanging off of a line of suits. It was a picture of Kira! I couldn't believe it. Up until then, she hadn't said a word about modeling; this is how I actually found out. Yet here she was, the promotional image for a bikini manufacturer. How lucky could a guy be? You would think a beautiful young girl would have made that the first thing she said when she met a guy and was trying to impress him. But she never needed to brag. Even if she wasn't a professional model, she certainly looked like one. Being fairly young and impressionable at the time, I of course thought this was 'all so impressive', and certainly helped fill my head a bit.

Not only was she beautiful, but she was really sweet as well. She came from a big family, which I liked, since back home it was only me, Mom, Dad, and Marcel. I know if my parents hadn't had problems doing so, we would have had a dozen kids. Kira's mother was British and her father Canadian. As time went by, I became close with her entire family. One of her older brothers, in particular, became one of my closest friends and as I was taking martial arts training in Toronto, I eventually got him into it as well when he, Kira, and I were living in Toronto.

In addition to the modeling, Kira spent a lot of time taking acting classes. She also got herself a degree in English. At one time, she thought about becoming a writer. As life evolved for both of us, she decided to learn more about business and got licensed as an institutional investment trader. I don't know if that was ever her passion, but it did pay well. Once we moved to Ottawa, she got involved in design advertising. She'd always had a good eye for art, and now with a background in both business as well as modeling, which she did for the advertising industry, this seemed like a nice melding of her interests and talents.

We dated for several years. She came for a year to my last year University at UNB, and lived off campus with a good friend of mine 'Bubba', Mike Gould, and 2 others in a large house we called 'the White House'. We then moved to Toronto when I started working at IBM, and she continued her University degree there in parallel. Eventually we got married, and I could not have been happier. We talked about having children, but we were both spending an awful lot of time on our career tracks, me in particular, and so we kept putting it off. We both wanted to be able to dedicate a good amount of time and energy into being parents.

Once we'd been together about ten years, Kira suddenly started to have a variety of health problems. We had noticed little things over a two-year period. Some manifested themselves as purely physical, while others seemed to affect her mind, her mood, and her overall being. It concerned her and it concerned me as well. We went to every doctor we could find. The thing with doctors is that each one seems to have a different idea of what the problem is as well as what is the solution. Sometimes I think they're just too scared to admit they haven't a clue sometimes and are flinging things against a wall, looking to see what will stick. There's actually a medical philosophy to that – where the reaction to treatment defines the malady. The problem was, the whole situation was being dragged out and dragged out because it was never "just take this one pill and by tomorrow you should be fine … or not." Every treatment involved something that had to be tried for six months or so before we could anticipate any positive reaction at all. That meant for six months you either had to deal with a worsening condition brought on by unwanted side effects, or simply a continuation of what had been the problem all along. It was very sad for both of us.

We were soon both losing faith in the doctors we had tried as well as doctors in general. We started consulting "Dr. Internet" to see what he might lead us to. The more we read, the more we started to suspect she had a brain tumor. This is, of course, very serious stuff, and our anxiety grew and grew.

We took our concerns to the doctor we were seeing at the time – Doctor #3 – but he pooh-poohed it by saying, "Well, Doctor #2 already ruled that out." Our response was that we felt Doctor #2 had only ruled it out theoretically, rather than going through a total workup of scans and so forth. It was quite the debate, but in the end the doctor agreed to run the tests. Sure enough, the scans were positive: Kira had a brain tumor. And sadly, we had diagnosed it first, not the doctors.

We were devastated. Like most people, we heard the phrase, "brain tumor" and thought, "fatal." She was so young. On the other hand, after having been to four doctors, been poked and probed a hundred different ways, been on every medication under the sun, and suffered through all the maladies which caused us to try all these things in the first place, there was actually a bit of a ray of sunshine in simply knowing what the heck had actually been the problem all along.

We found a surgeon in Toronto who was considered the best around. The tumor was on her frontal lobe and this surgeon was experimenting with less invasive procedures where he went up through the gum line or nasal cavity rather than shaving the head and sawing open the skull – called *transsphenoidal* surgery. The concept was more appealing to us both, particularly to Kira. What woman wants her head shaved and a big scar on her scalp?

I took three weeks off from work. We were living in Ottawa at the time, but I more or less moved to Toronto for the duration of the hospitalization and recovery. We spent day and night together. I would never leave her side.

Emotions run high during times like these. It's like you're on a constant adrenaline rush. You're not yourself. People around you say things and do things and your mind is going a mile a minute, trying to process it all while worrying about other things at the very same time. Amidst this confusion, the doctor started rattling off some potential side effects of this type of surgery, working around the frontal lobe, etc. Well heck, there are potential side effects to everything. We'd had to listen to this litany with every single medication that had been tried on Kira. We were almost becoming jaded; we only half listened to the doctor's warnings. They're nothing but a laundry list of possible problems and who's to say which, if any, of the myriad of things might possibly happen?

In our case, one of the things lightly mentioned in passing when discussing expectations of post-surgery elements, was that Kira had a very small percentage chance to awaken from surgery with a 'slight alteration' to her personality. The frontal lobe includes the controls for personality and here we were about to mess with it. Still, when your wife has a brain tumor, you don't think, "Hey, all these potential problems that could arise while trying to remove it – primary among them death – aren't they all miniature in comparison to the inevitable death one would be sentenced to by simply letting it go and doing nothing?" Looking back, I'm sure we would have done nothing differently. She was suffering and she needed surgery, period.

The surgery was successful. I fell on my knees in thanks. They got all of it. Medically, she was expected to make a full recovery. We both could not be happier.

We packed our things and moved back to Ottawa and I returned to my job. Around this same time we were looking for a new house. My job was doing well and money was flowing. Outside of Kira's health problems, life was good. And now, now with her tumor removed, these should have been the good times.

We found a great, big new house. All I thought about was that Kira would be getting better and better by the day and soon we would be able to start a family together, which is why the bigger house was something we wanted.

We were in the new house about three weeks when Kira felt up to going back to work herself. By then we had also made some acquaintances around our new neighborhood. A couple named Connie and Bill, retirees who lived next door, seemed like nice people and we decided to invite them over for dinner. I liked Connie and Bill, as they liked to walk our dog Roxy a lot, which was fine for me as poor Roxy, a Jack Russell, needed far more exercise that we had the time to provide, unfortunately.

It's funny, but as I look back, it was one of the best moments in my life. I loved my job. I was making good money. Everything seemed to be on the upswing. Kira had been through hell but now she was well.

She was even going back to work. We had this big new house, which I wanted to fill with children. When you're an adopted kid, being a parent means a lot. I loved my mom and dad and they raised me with such love. Now I wanted to pass that love along to someone else. And here we were, meeting some nice folks from the neighborhood and inviting them over. It was such a classic, family scene. What could go wrong?

Kira came home from work and went immediately upstairs. This didn't faze me at all. The truth was, during the time when she had the tumor, Kira frequently exhibited erratic behavior. It was the tumor on the frontal lobe that was causing it. At times it was exasperating, prior to knowing the cause. We had unusual conversations a lot and I felt badly for my part in that, since it really wasn't Kira's fault; it was her tumor talking. As her diagnosis became apparent to us both, I became far more tolerant and always tried to let things go, no matter what came out of her mouth or what she did. It wasn't her; it was the tumor. That became our mantra. Thus, I had almost forgotten that the operation was supposed to make these quirks go away. It had only been a few weeks since the operation and when she still occasionally acted a bit off, I continued to ignore it. It wasn't her; it was the tumor. Except there no longer was a tumor, which I had conveniently forgotten since I was so happy my wife was healthy once more.

Connie and Bill were to come over soon and Kira was still upstairs. No problem, no big deal. I can cook – sort of – and I had pasta boiling on the stove top. I also make a pretty mean Carbonara sauce, so things were looking up.

Kira came down and I gave her the lowdown on the progress of the meal. I was a happy camper, but the look on her face was rather flat and without affect. "We have to talk," she said. Who hasn't heard those words before? But I was in a great mood. As I said, it was one of the best periods of my life and nothing could get me down, or so I thought.

She looked at me and said, "I've been thinking; I don't want to have kids anymore." Okay, that took me back a bit, but then I quickly rationalized to myself, 'This is Kira. She's been erratic like this for two years or more. It's the tumor talking, even with the tumor gone. She's still recovering and she's still not 100% herself. I'll let it slide as I have everything else and we'll see how it develops. By tomorrow she may have forgotten she'd even said it.' The thing is, telling me we wouldn't have kids together was about the worst thing I could have possibly heard, but again, I couldn't take her seriously. I'd learned not to take things that came out of her mouth too seriously when the tumor was at its worst. During the worst of her days with the tumor, she'd said some absolutely crazy things. I would absorb it, and simply tell her things will get better and move past trying not to assume there was any logic to the statements. The next day things would be fine, and the cycle would repeat itself soon. Saying she didn't want kids was mild and banal in comparison.

"Fine, no problem. We'll talk some more about it tomorrow," I said, brushing it off, as I stirred the sauce. Nothing was going to get me down tonight.

"No, it's more than that. I don't want to be married and I'm going to leave tomorrow."

Okay, that one made me stop stirring the sauce. I didn't know what to say and I still tried to give her the benefit of the doubt. This couldn't be her talking; it was the tumor, it was the frontal lobe. I tried to brush it off as nicely as possible, although she was killing my buzz a bit.

"I don't want to be married and I'm leaving tomorrow," she repeated. With that she turned around and went back upstairs. The doorbell rang at that instant before I had time to really process this with any seriousness, and I went to let in Connie and Bill, who came into the kitchen, and I made them a drink. I don't know if they could see how rattled I was. I simply said Kira was upstairs changing and would be down soon, which I sort of believed would be the case, as her behavior and attitude could switch that abruptly as a result of the tumor's side affects.

I poured the neighbors a drink and made small talk. They were nice folks and we sat together on high stools in the kitchen as the sauce simmered on low heat, chatting about lighthearted subjects. I figured that would buy us both some time until she snapped out of her mood and came back downstairs to be neighborly. The next thing I know, I heard her come downstairs, then heard the front door slam, followed by dead silence. Kira was gone, gone without another word.

I never saw her again.

I didn't know what was happening at the time. I somehow got through dinner. The neighbors were swell about it. I made up some excuse; what it was I can't remember and it's unimportant. But dinner came and went, the night came and went, and my wife was missing completely. When she didn't come home at all that night, it began to ache in my brain that maybe she wasn't going to wait until tomorrow to leave me, as she had threatened.

I called her family. They knew nothing. As days went by, I continued to call her family. They were now as worried as me. Kira had always had a close relationship with her mother; by this time her father had already passed away some years prior. Just as suddenly, she stopped talking to her own family as often as she used to. When she was finally found, she had cut off her long hair to sport a new style. She changed the way she dressed to a completely different look. She got rid of her cat. Every single thing about her personality shifted. I heard she may have even got rid of her cat, although not verified. Most of the main elements of her personality simply shifted. I told myself that it must have been completely related to the tumor and surgery affects, and nothing to do with my own contributions to our relationship. This was convenient to think, as trying to add up my many fallibilities did not seem like the best self-therapy at the time. It wasn't simply aberrant behavior. She quit her job and started another. She, quite simply, was no longer Kira. She was not insane or anything like that. All I can liken it to is if someone you knew one day just became a completely other person. Every aspect of her personality changed. That "by the way comment" from the Doctor that came before her operation now took on a much greater significance. "A smaller percent chance of a slight personality shift" was what he said as I recall. This was to be the largest slight of my life.

Furthermore, what she seemed to desire most was to cut off all ties with the old Kira – her family, her husband, her career. She wanted nothing in her life that reminded her of the life she had led up until that very moment. She dismissed it all. I'd never seen anything like it before and I hope I never do. The very brief conversation I had with the doctor prior to the operation, where amongst two dozen other facts before signing release papers on the operation, he had mentioned a small percent chance of a "personality shift" following a procedure like this. Of course I had no idea the probability or significance of that statement at the time; who would? All I knew was that I wanted her better, to get that tumor out right now.

She had brothers and sisters and they managed to see her occasionally, but they got the same impression as her mother and I did. This person was not Kira. It was like "Invasion of the Body Snatchers" or a witness protection program of some sort. She'd ditched her entire being and swapped it for a new one.

Kira and I had been together for almost 10 years. Perhaps, had it been a shorter relationship, I might have gotten over it faster, but I was completely devastated. For the first two weeks she was gone, I could not focus to work. I stayed at home a couple days and a couple times laid on the floor in a fetal position and felt like I was dead. I prayed in every which way a man could, down on my hands and knees begging God to change this thing around as I was massively confused, yet nothing stopped the trajectory she was on. Before, she'd had "episodes." This was not an episode. She seemed changed for good and the person she'd become wanted nothing to do with me, for no discernable reason. Most relationships, when they end, there's fighting, there are issues; maybe someone is caught cheating. None of these things had happened – it was so abrupt that it was almost like she had been abducted or killed to me. Perhaps if they had it wouldn't have hurt so badly. Instead, it was as if the surgery had simply killed her, had stolen her away from me forever. I often wonder, if both of us had known that would have been the case, would we have both agreed to take that direction medically? You get surgery to save a life. We had saved a life, but it seemed like it was someone else's, not Kira's.

Once I got off the floor and went back to work, I was still a mess. For the entire first year without Kira, I couldn't bring myself to date. The thought of being with another woman sickened me. Although divorce proceedings commenced, in my mind we were still married. It didn't matter that I wasn't with her and I couldn't see her. We were still Mike and Kira and that was that. Needless to say, I was a lost soul, stumbling around, trying to bury myself in my work and dreading going home only to discover Kira was not there and never would be again.

After a year, guys started to bug me to go out on dates. They were being nice and trying to be supportive, but I still wasn't ready. Nonetheless, I tried to follow their good-hearted prodding and got fixed up on a few dates. It must have been hell for those other women. All I could talk about was Kira. Who wants to listen to that? I was a complete downer. I needed more time to heal.

Finally, I dated a couple times until I eventually did meet a woman who appeared to be exactly what I needed. She was an assistant vice president in research and development. We were in the same industry. We met a few times purely for business. Me, I was still too damaged to notice she was looking at me as something other than a colleague. She was creating excuses for us to see one another, which, if I'd been more cognizant, would have flattered me, but I was initially clueless. Eventually, when we couldn't arrange office meetings because of our schedules, she suggested drinks after work. Again, like a slightly clueless dolt, I accepted, not thinking anything of it.

Looking back, though, I was still not ready for a relationship. I was an open sore, one of the walking wounded. People need to be healthy when they commit to another and I was as far from emotionally healthy as one could be. I was still in mourning over someone else. But now I'd become needy, far needier than I'd ever been before. This new woman seemed to want the same things I wanted out of life and she was aggressive about getting them. One problem though: They weren't even necessarily the things I wanted right at that moment in my life. They were the things I'd wanted for Kira and I. When I was with this new woman, it was like I was imagining I was back with Kira. I could pick up where I'd left off. We could be like I'd imagined Kira and I would be once she'd been released from the hospital. This of course was evidence I was not quite ready for a new relationship frankly. To add to my already cloudy thinking, I received news of my father getting cancer.

In essence, I was lost in my own head. This was totally unfair to the new woman in my life, but I was too wrapped up in my blues to realize what was happening to me. For her part, this lady wanted all of the things I'd wanted Kira to want, and she wanted them now, just as I'd hoped Kira would. My new courtship seemed to be in fast forward, as she felt we should quickly move in together, and soon thereafter indicated since her Visa for working in Canada would soon expire after being laid off, marriage would help allow our relationship to continue this fast momentum. I wanted to have back what I had with Kira. We married after a very, very short courtship.

Mistake. She already had a daughter from a previous marriage and said she wanted more family right away. Hey I wanted a family right away, too, and as such she immediately became pregnant on our Hawaiian honeymoon actually. We had not discussed it being 'that fast', as I wasn't even aware she was going off birth control. Over the next few months, I kept looking to her for similar connection as I had before. Unfortunately, none of them existed, and what became clearer as the clouds cleared for me, was person that was simply far too different from me to make a marriage work. She wasn't Kira, in many ways. Her personality was very controlling and stroppy, and those tendencies made it very difficult for me to adjust. The thing is, I wasn't ready for this new woman, or for any woman, really. I wanted a connection like I experienced before. The problem is, I only began to realize this once it was too late. We were already married and now we were expecting a child.

I tried to make the best of it, but we were failing. The more time we spent together, the more apparent it became that we were a complete and utter mismatch. We never should have gotten together in the first place. I accept as much fault in that as could be. For her part, she seemed to know what she wanted at that stage in her life, and was determined to accept only the image of what she wanted, no less at any cost. We weren't right for each other and our own selfish needs at the time blinded us to the obvious.

Nine months after we said "I do," my beautiful daughter Alexandra was born. While the marriage was not a success by any standard, Alexandra had become the single greatest achievement of my life, hands down. I thought this might rescue us from our divisions, but it did not. As I said, we were a mismatch; we never should have been together in the first place and even my angel Alexandra wasn't going to change that. When she was only six months old, I couldn't take the volatility anymore. I filed for divorce.

When a relationship breaks up, it's easy to blame the other party. With Kira, I can't even bring myself to blame her and I certainly cannot blame myself. It was a medical problem and there was nothing either of us could do about it. Once she was cured, with the personality shift as a result, she did not want me and there was nothing I could change about myself to make myself into the person she wanted. In that sense, neither of us was at fault. With my new partner, I suppose we were both at fault to some degree. Nonetheless, both relationships were over and here I was, in the eyes of the world, a two-time loser. I hated myself for that. I'd grown up in a Catholic household, raised to believe that love was forever, and yet both of my marriages had ended in divorce. For all the professional accomplishments of my life, those two divorces hung around my neck like millstones. They shamed and embarrassed me.

Now I had a daughter and no wife. My daughter's mother was actually an American citizen, working in Canada on a visa. She was originally from Texas. Once we divorced, she wanted to go back to the States. Where would this leave me? I loved our baby more than anything else in the world. I'd always wanted a child. Even though this had all happened so fast and had happened, apparently, with the wrong person, that still did not have any effect on the fact I now had a child.

Right before coming to Canada, she had worked in Raleigh, North Carolina. She'd made a number of friends there and she had an entrée to return to work back in that area. I stayed in Canada for the next year, working for BreconRidge, but the fact I had a little baby which I had to travel thousands of miles to see was simply killing me.

I started looking around Raleigh for a job, but then she started talking about moving back to Texas, where her family was. This left me in total confusion. Where was I to go? If I took a job in Raleigh, she might just up and go to Texas and then what would I do? It's one thing to job hop. It's another to do it over and over again in a short period of time. And just because I'd been doing well career-wise, that didn't mean I could just pick any city on a world map and know I could find a job there equal or better to the one I already had. I did know that being closer to my daughter Alexandra was more important to me than any job, so I resolved to make that happen.

I pulled the trigger and moved to Texas, pulling up stakes and finding a good job for myself down there. Again, I knew my ex and our daughter were not there yet, but I assumed they might eventually end up there from what I was hearing in discussions with her on longer term plans. Either way, I was now closer to her, with an ability to have more frequent and consistent visits, without the added cost and hassles of crossing a border. You would have thought by now I would have learned all about what happens when people "assume." I mean, it made perfect sense to me. She was from Texas and she still had family there. She was now a single mom and single moms need help, love, and support and who is better to provide that than family?

Irony of ironies, I moved to Texas, and lived there for 8 years, and my ex never ended up moving back. I was surrounded there by people with funny accents (to me) who, upon meeting *me*, actually say, "Boy, y'all got a funny accent. Where you from?"

I can't complain too much, though. I went to work for, a global contract electronics manufacturing company called Flextronics, as the VP Americas in Operations. Along with some other sites in the US, Canada and Mexico reporting to me, ended up also having three factories in the Carolinas, so I would get to go out there a lot and when I did, I would spend as much time with Alexandra as possible. We saw each other at least once a month. My ex ended up cycling though several jobs, and one layoff too many she started to look outside NC. New relationships with other men led her to Wyoming, then another in Minnesota, so I chased my daughter around for some time in trying to maintain my monthly visit ritual with her. At the time of completing this book, some 8 years after starting with Flextronics, I then transitioned to a new role with a growing force in the 'online store' space called Amazon.com, where I decided to join them as VP North American Regional Operations & Engineering. At this point I had taken full custody of Alexandra while in Texas, now living with me, where she went to a private Montessori school until we moved to Seattle later that year. Once in Seattle, she loved it, but was even more thrilled to finally lose the formal Montessori School uniform!

CHAPTER FIVE

STARTING TO SEARCH – PRE-GOOGLE

"Man, know thyself."

Socrates

It's an itch that never really goes away. You go about your life – education, love, career, finding yourself. It's in that last one – finding yourself – that tends to rear its head the most. When most people start thinking introspectively, they consider a ton of things – who am I? Why do I do the things I do? Am I likeable? Do *I* like myself? What do I really want out of life? Part of all this involves looking back at our personal past. What lessons have we learned along the way? How did I get here? Am I repeating certain mistakes I've made before? If so, how can I break the chain and move forward instead of laterally?

For kids raised in the environment of their natural parents, there is also the analysis of who are these people I call "Mom" and "Dad?" Yes, even we adoptees think of that as well, but when we do, we only tend to take it just so far. It's the whole "nature versus nurture" argument. I look at my mom and dad and think, "She's like this and so am I;" "Dad's like this, which is where I must get that other thing from." But then you hit a wall. You snap-to and realize you have been heavily influenced by these two people, yet for adoptees you are not the blood of their blood. There are things within you that focusing upon your adoptive parents cannot explain. We all do certain things unlike our parents. It's natural. We are children, not clones. But when that happens to most kids, it can just be written off as "Well, I guess that part is just me being me," or else maybe it's a trait of old Grandpa Smith or Crazy Aunt Edith. But when you're adopted, you see something about yourself that is unlike the people who raised you and you think, "Is this me, or am I repeating something unique to the people who created me biologically?" It plays with your mind. Sometimes, it becomes a convenient scapegoat for you. Do something bad, something you later regret, and you think,

"Maybe it's not my fault. Maybe the reason I do that is because of my birth father." There were even times when ever I would hit a particularly rough patch in my childhood, which all kids do from time to time, however I would go to sleep at night sometimes and dream about the life I would envision my life was "supposed" to be. I would be falling into a slumber thinking I was really in a deep sleep all this time, and I would soon awake to realize what I thought was my real life was really just a bad dream - and I would wake up and all would be better. And I would dream about how different life would be in my parallel life. Perhaps it was a really a coping mechanism that the imaginative young mind is gifted with.

The bottom line is, it plagues you. Maybe not every day, maybe not even every week or every month. But as you mature and grow, you think more about it. You think about it when you're alone with your thoughts. You wonder. You wish at times that you could just meet your biologicals somehow, someway, just so you can figure yourself out a little bit better.

I was pretty nonchalant about all this throughout my youth. A lot of adoptees go through self-pitying, overly-dramatic moments, especially when the hormones are raging, but this was never the case with me – at least not for that reason. But once I went away to university that began to change. Again, I would not bring any self-pity into the equation, simply self-awareness and self-exploration. Maturity. To be mature is to ask questions. I asked questions, although many of them were questions even my parents had no answers to. I also asked questions internally. I thought deeper, as well I should have.

What religion was I? College kids think about that a lot. In our youth, we go to the church or mosque or temple that our parents go to. We adopt their belief system because it is the only one we know. By college, kids start to think more independently. But for an adoptee, there is that little extra twist. I had been raised Catholic. I'd been led to believe my birth parents were Catholic, too. But were they? What if they weren't? What if they'd been Jewish? Would I have been betraying their lineage – *my* lineage – all these years by turning my back on my true faith? Who knows? More so however, were thoughts about who my birth parents were as people, what was "their story," and what did they look like.

I'd stare into the mirror longer than before. Yes, when you're in your late teens and early twenties you become far more vein, but it was more than that. I knew I didn't look like my mother or father. Never did. It never bothered me before and it still didn't. What did bother me, though, was looking at myself and wondering, "Well, then, who the hell *do* I look like?"

Confidence. I'd never really lacked it before, nor did I lack it then, but deep inside, mine was being rocked somewhat. A person who knows who they are, who knows their family and their parents, knows a lot about the path they are embarking on as adults. What about my health history? At least once a year I would fill out some sort of health questionnaire that asked, "Is there any history of heart disease in your family?" If so, maybe I'd needed to be far more careful than the next guy when it came to eating healthfully. Was there addiction? In my early years I would like to knock back a few beers as much as most guys, but might I be more susceptible to overdoing it because of some biological predisposition? I did not know, and for the first time in my life it worried me. I felt there were all these potential pitfalls out there waiting for me, as there are for everyone, but in my case, I was flying blind. It's not a good feeling. It made me feel that others had some sort of advantage in life over me. I just wanted to connect to that same thread of life as others, and know that face in the mirror a little better.

> "I just wanted to connect to that same thread of life as others, and know that face in the mirror a little better."

In Canada, you can register your name with the government as an adoptee. If your birth mother at some point does the same, the authorities can connect the dots for you. In other words, I knew my date of birth and my place of birth, as well as my gender, obviously. If my mother voluntarily registered as well, she would list that same information. Put all that data together and if you didn't hook the two pieces up perfectly, you'd come darn close. I mean, how many white male babies were born in Saint John on that very day in that very year and were put up for adoption? Not too many, I had to imagine. Heck, I might have been the only one. The only problem was, this only worked if my mother also registered, and there was no law compelling her to do so.

I registered my name with the government agency handling adoption records in the late 80s. With high hopes being the fool they are, I somehow expected that I'd hear something back in just a matter of days. That could only have happened had my mother registered before I did. And so I waited and waited. It finally became clear to me that she had not yet registered. I waited some more. Waiting can drive you crazy. You start to think of the world being in some sort of vacuum where the only thing going on is this, that I could send some sort of psychic signal to some woman somewhere and somehow she would know it and sign up to find me. It's even more ridiculous than waiting for a deadbeat's check to come in the mail. I was waiting for a check from a person who didn't even know they owed me one!

As time went by, it became a comedy of errors. I had later been told that a reason for the delays in getting back to me on whether or not my birth mother had registered was because the building where the original records for me were stored had burned down, and information regarding my records had been transferred to microfiche. This meant the data analysts had that much harder a time in tracing information. Of course, the Internet of today has made searching for information so much more transparent and simpler now. I couldn't believe that. Crazy.

By the time I moved to Toronto, I was even more absorbed in this mini-drama of my own making. Kira and I wanted children. For a lot of adoptees, that's when the dinner bell goes off. I wanted kids. Did I have any inheritable diseases? Was I carrying something? It's not fair to my offspring, nor is it fair to my wife for us not to know. But that's the situation we were in.

The registration system wasn't working for me. I'd given it years by now. What was left for me to do? I was making some money now, so I thought, "Why not hire a private detective?" Sure, it might sound a little drastic, but it wasn't prohibitively expensive for me and I really, really wanted some answers. Even my mom was excited at the possibility this could bring, as she was at this point actively engaged in helping me search from several angles. It was really great to have her support in searching for my birth parent history.

The person I hired was a woman and this was her particular specialty. In only two weeks, she came back to me with some leads. I was so impressed. All this time I'd been just waiting and waiting and in no time at all, this woman was already well on the trail.

"I think I may have found the family," she said. "There's this family named 'Wilband' and there are a bunch of sisters. I just need to find out their ages and from that I should be able to determine which one is the mother." She asked that I give her another week or so and she would come back to me with more definitive information on who exactly the mother may be.

To this day I really don't know exactly how she did what she did in such a short time. I guess that's why she gets paid for what she does. She went through public records and hospital records, armed with my birth date, and somehow concluded that someone named Wilband gave birth on that day and year in Saint John. Could she have been wrong? Yes, I'm sure there was a chance. I mean, my date and place of birth were all taken on faith, and if that data was wrong, I don't know where we would have gone from there. But for as much as it was a private adoption without disclosure, I suppose my birth mother had no paranoid desire to cover things up as if she were some Soviet spy or something. She delivered in a hospital, not at home, and she used her real name, not an alias, or so we presumed.

Could I have gotten all this information on our own, I don't know.

Maybe the woman I hired slipped some secretary a little tip to look the other way while she rifled through some old records; how do I know? I neither know nor do I care. I'm about results. Nonetheless, I felt I was suddenly getting so close to the truth that I was damn near salivating.

As I mentioned, the detective asked for one more week to follow up on all this, to determine whether her tip was legit and if it was, which Wilband woman was the correct one. In our initial finding call, she had rattled off some more details – there was a Louise in Florida, a Joan in Phoenix, a Ruth in Des Moines, and an Agnes in Saint John. Naturally, I jumped a little hearing there was one in Saint John, but the detective felt that the Saint John woman had the least likelihood of being the one, in her humble opinion. Still, my reaction was typical. We always tend to assume things occur in a vacuum; that nothing changes and that people remain where they began, forever and ever, amen. All the same, we contradict our own preconceptions, moving about as so many of us do. I was in Toronto at the time. If someone went looking for me in Saint John, they wouldn't have found me there, either.

The one in Saint John she could more easily gather information on, and the detective felt that this lady simply seemed too old and I should dismiss her as a possibility. But I continued to get the detective talking, curious as I was. In the process, I got her to give up the last names of these women as well. They'd all married and had new monikers now, so this was important. That's what always makes it easier to find men in this world. We always keep our same last names.

I've never been a sit-and-stay-put kind of guy. I tend to be high energy and very driven. For me to now just squat like a bump on a log waiting another week for this woman I'd hired to complete her task was just too much for me. No disrespect to her, but I was too excited now. I felt as if I'd waited my entire life for the answer that was about to come and now I was like the kid who knows his Christmas presents are hidden in Mom and Dad's closet. It was too damn tempting to not want to sneak in and take a look-see.

I called directory assistance and asked for a number for the first name on the list as I had written it: Louise of Florida. No, I should not have done it. I was wrong. But I was going a little crazy and I simply could not sit still.

A woman answered and I said, "Louise, you don't know me, but my name is Michael and I was born in Saint John." I gave her the day and year to see if that alone might shock her into a response, but nothing was imminent. I continued. "I was put up for adoption and I have some reason to believe that someone in your family might be my mother." I tried to say this all with a gentle, non-aggressive tone. I had no quarrel with anyone and I certainly wasn't trying to be accusatory. I went on to say, "I've been searching for many years and if I'm completely off the mark or if I'm making you at all uncomfortable, I apologize."

She responded in kind. "No, no problem. I don't mind at all. I can tell you this, though: it's not me. But, you know, I don't doubt it's one of my sisters. We have a very eclectic family and we moved to all different cities. It wouldn't surprise me if one of them did it and I didn't know all about it firsthand." Of course, as I was hearing this, I knew nothing of just *how* eclectic the Wilband girls had been and what sorts of adventures they'd had with boyfriends, other women's husbands, adoptions, abortions, and what-not.

Louise took some pauses and I realized she was thinking hard. If I strained, I could almost hear her mumbling to herself, "It could have been Joan ... or maybe Ruth. If it was in Saint John, it might have been ..." and on and on. It didn't seem like an act to me. It appeared I'd actually hit the right family; it was simply a matter of getting the right girl.

She asked for my name and number and she promised me she would look further into this and if she discovered something, she promised to call me back. She sounded sincere and I appreciated it greatly. I felt I had made a quantum leap in only the course of that one phone call. I was getting close, so darn close; I was just certain of it.

I was tempted to call the other sisters, but I was almost too excited now. Sometimes you have to just trust that the wheels of progress will turn without you having to make them move all by your lonesome. Patience. I don't claim to have a lot of it, but I was at least attempting it.

It was 1993; easy to remember because the Blue Jays were in the World Series and the Series was going on right at this very same time – October. I watched every game and rooted for my Jays, but aside from that, I had this new excitement in my life.

One night I'm at this Irish pub owned by the Irish Rovers, the great musical group, watching the game with some buddies from work. The bar was called The Unicorn and it was on Eglington near Young Street in Toronto. A great place to hang with the boys and watch a ballgame on one of the TVs in the quaint atmosphere it provided.

Suddenly, early on in the evening, Kira comes running into the bar. She finds me and says, "Mike, I have to make this quick. I'm double-parked out front, but I knew you'd want to know. Your mom called!"

My mom and I talked all the time. It's no big deal. I couldn't imagine why this would prompt her to come interrupt a world series game, so I simply said, "Tell her I'm watching the game, I'll call her later." Then she looks at me like I'm the biggest dummy in the world and says, "No, your *birth* mother – Ruth!"

Ruth? Who the hell was Ruth? Apparently, Louise Wilband had called around to her other sisters and had found the one who said, "Yes, that would be *my* child." That must have been a series of very strange phone calls, but I wouldn't really grasp onto that until much later. Nor at this moment would I stop and overanalyze what was before me. I took Kira at her word and my adrenaline shot up sky high. Who else but my real, biological mother would magically manage to get my home phone number and call it such a short time after I had spoken to this Louise woman in Florida?

I was stunned. Kira continued. "She just called and we talked and she started crying and I started crying and it was incredible." My jaw was agape. Kira went on. "We talked for a long time. She told me all about you and how she regretted giving you up. She said she thinks about you all of the time, especially around your birthday." Kira continued to recall what had gone on between her and this woman, but I had trouble paying attention to it. All that I faced were the headlines: My mother was alive. She had been found. I would soon find out who exactly I was. All these years, and now, finally, I would know.

I was torn. I mean, the Jays were in the process of winning the World Series, for crying out loud! Joe Carter was hitting home runs to end games on one swing of the bat and things like that. On top of that, Toronto is no place to double-park. They don't just ticket you in Toronto. They first slap a huge ticket on your windshield, and in addition they then tow your car to one of many distant car lots. Usually, you first think your car was stolen, then once you take an hour to call several tow lots to see if they have your car. It is freakin stressful. The local traffic cops are not laid-back, patient and forgiving people, despite what you may know or have heard about us Canadians as a whole.

I told Kira to quickly jump back in the car before it got towed and I would finish my beer and head home. I mean, I was excited as hell, but this was Toronto about to win the World Series! I might never get to see this sort of thing again. So I then finished my drink, and then - ordered another. I then headed home with a bizarre mixture of emotions rushing through me.

Me, I'd taken a cab to the bar – I *knew* how tough it was to park around there – and I flagged one down for my return home. When I walked in, Kira was still in a state of high spirits, still freaking out a bit. We'd had a very close marriage before she got sick. We lived and died on each other's triumphs and tragedies, and this one was a whopper.

There on the desk was Ruth's phone number, which she left with Kira. I stared at it for a while. This whole thing was becoming almost too much for me as well. It was like staring at a winning lottery ticket. Sure, it's your dream come true, but for a moment – I can only imagine, since I've never had the pleasure or the luck – you stare at it, almost afraid to cash it in. You think about how your entire life is about to change completely once you go to the claim center. Once you do it, or in my case once I made that phone call, things will never be the same.

We all waste a lot of moments in life. They pass us by and we don't even think about them probably until we're on our deathbed, recollecting the things we never did or the people we never told how much we loved them. And then there are the moments you *know* you'll never forget, like when your baby is being born, or when you graduate from college or you ask a girl to marry you. This was one of those moments.

I grabbed the number and I called. As I heard it ringing on her end, it occurred to me I had no idea what I was going to say. No prepared speech. I wish I *had* prepared something, but I'd jumped the gun and there was no turning back now.

In those heart-shaking milliseconds, I tried to conjure up her voice. I imagined it as being not that much different from mine – a voice belonging to someone perhaps fourteen, fifteen, or sixteen years older than me, not much more. Your typical pregnant teen who knew she had to give up her baby in order to finish high school. It's a stereotype and that's what we're raised on – stereotypes. When my adopted mom and dad, Joan and Rene, had approached Catholic Welfare in the first place looking to adopt, their laundry list of what they wanted in a mother was just like that: a young girl, healthy, bright, and Catholic, for that was also very important to them. Catholic Welfare, for their part, promised her they would deliver on all that and once they placed me in my mother's arms, they swore that was my heritage. In essence, from what I gathered, they at the time handed to you what you wanted to hear.

The phone picked up on the other end and I heard, instead, an elderly voice. Strange. I almost wanted to ask for the woman's daughter, but my mind wasn't working that quickly. I said tentatively, "Ruth?" The elderly voice said, "Hello!" That threw me for a loop. As soon as I identified myself, her voice started cracking with emotion. She was very, very nervous, which only made me less nervous, thank God. I immediately began consoling her, and not really having thought about what I would first say if and when I would find her, an instinctual response came out. "Look, Ruth, I gotta thank you for calling me, I take it Louise and you talked. It's been a very long journey for me. But before we talk about anything, I'd just like to do one thing first, and that is to thank you for the decision you made to bring me into this world. I know you had other choices."

With that she started crying and I could just tell how she must have been feeling. When she collected herself, she said, "You've taken a lot of weight off of my shoulders. I think about you every year on your birthday." She said once again what she had said to Kira during their cry session.

We're all a bit self-centered in life. When we die, it's just us in the casket. Here I was, thinking only of my own needs and my own personal curiosities throughout this process. I'd hardly spent a minute considering what her life had been like and what she'd been through until that very moment. I only began to consider how she'd feel being tapped out of the blue by me right around the time I was waiting for her to answer when I called her.

We talked a lot, covering just about everything either of us could possibly think of. It must have gone on for about an hour and a half. She told me about the guy she originally thought was my father. He was an executive at New York Telephone. Believe it or not, we didn't dwell too much on that. We were mostly talking about her, which was fine by me because I wanted to know everything – *everything* – about her. She went on and on about her family. It was obvious right from the start that they were all quite close, her sisters and she, as well as their husbands, her nieces and nephews and so on. The names were flying at me fast and furiously and I struggled to keep up and scribbling notes on a small piece of paper. I suppose she was still high on all the excitement of the moment and couldn't stop talking, just as I couldn't stop listening.

I wish I would have taken better notes, and vowed to do so in the future, if we were to speak again as I couldn't find the cryptic transcript that I did take that night. My head was spinning with emotion as well as information. Perhaps this is another reason why I didn't push too hard on the issue of who my father was. The facts and stories were flying at me so fast I felt like a guy in a batting cage who had neither a bat nor a helmet.

I was just trying to survive and get through it all. Only once I was done did I assess my own performance and find some of it lacking, hoping I would get a do-over sometime soon so I could slow everything down and squeeze from her tales the things that were most important to me.

As I played it all back in my mind after I hung up, it struck me how certain she was that she was mine and I was hers. The thing is, when she put me up for adoption, she had already named me: Michael Thomas Wilband. My mother who raised me, my real mother, had already told me that when she received me I was already named Michael and that the only thing she and my dad did was change my middle name to Rene, after my dad. Ruth's story, then, was checking out. On the other hand Marcel, my brother, had a completely different name when he was put up for adoption and my parents had changed it to Joseph Marcel. Mom had told me, though, that she liked the name "Michael," so she kept it. In her mind it was a good, biblical name, and it went well with my new surname "Doiron."

Ruth and I exchanged addresses and promised to send each other pictures. I couldn't wait to see what she looked like. I promised her I would also call again soon, and thanked her for making the leap to return my call and inquired to her sister.

No sooner did she get my first letter with my picture in it did she call me. She said, "Michael, I made a mistake. Your father is another man. His name is Harter." I vaguely recollected her mentioning the name "Harter" in our first phone conversation, but I didn't recall immediately who or what he was to her. She continued, "As soon as I saw your photo, I knew; I just knew. You're the spitting image of him. I knew it *could* have been him, but I wasn't sure and was confused when you called me. I don't know how I surmised you were this other guy's child, but I did and I just set that all aside in my mind all of these years. But no, you are absolutely, positively the son of Harter Hull. I would stake my life on it."

From there on she wrote me the entire Harter Hull story. Again, my head spun. It had only been about week or so and I'd just been settling in with the assumed knowledge of who my father was, but here it was and I was being switched around again.

I called her and we spoke more about this at length. It began to grow on me that some man named Harter Hull, a war hero to his hometown, was my real father. I found I could sit back and let Ruth rhapsodize all about him without me ever getting bored. I loved the stories. I couldn't get enough.

I asked her if she ever told Harter he may have had a son with her. She hesitantly said yes, but I immediately doubted her. First off, she had told me when she first spoke with me that I was the son of another man. How then could she have told Harter? It had to be one thing or the other.

It was the first time I caught her in what might be called a lie. Nonetheless, I was not angry with her over it. The more we spoke, the more I tried to put myself in her shoes, not just in regard to how she must be feeling today, but how she must have felt each and every step of the way. I'm not about to get all judgmental about her not knowing who exactly was the father, but still, it was what it was and I know it must have been hard to talk about, especially to me. People lie about sex; it's just that simple. Look at what happened with President Clinton in the US. It doesn't make it right, but it's a human thing.

The way she tenuously claimed to have told Harter about me made me believe she was simply answering that way in order to make me feel better. This, too, is a human frailty. We tell little white lies to folks in order to make them feel good or to spare their feelings. I got the impression she carried around an awful lot of guilt because of me and if I were to get angry with her for some reason or another and bolt from her life no sooner than I had entered it, it would have broken her heart for sure. So she told me certain things to make me feel better. I could live with that. So long as the large issues were truthfully told to me, I would be all right.

Throughout the time I was communicating with Ruth, I was sharing all my trials and tribulations with my own mother, the sweet lady who raised me. I felt no guilt about looking for and finding Ruth, nor did my mother feel any hurt that I was doing so – in fact she was excited about the journey as well. During the time when I was still in search of Ruth and had not yet found her, my mother was my most stalwart assistant, traveling around Saint John, going to offices, libraries, and medical facilities, reading microfiche, etc. She was really into it. There was nothing she would not do for me. She even interviewed with the private detective I hired. That's the sign of a confident, loving woman. She had no reason to be jealous of some new lady coming into my life. She knew how she had raised me and knew how I would always feel about her. She showed her love to me by helping me find out exactly who I was.

I discussed it all, too, with Marcel, which was interesting. He, of course, had led a childhood similar to mine. We were both adopted and we grew up in the same house with the same parents. Unlike me, he was still living in Saint John and most likely might have had an even easier time of it had he chosen to look for his own birth parents. He was actually working for my dad, doing storefront work like glazing and such. I, too, had helped out Dad in summer jobs as I was growing up, but it was Marcel who decided to stick with him and enter the "family business" for good.

Dad might not have had a great education, but he was a PhD from the School of Hard Knocks. Look around you and you will likely find a lot of guys like him, people who could have easily succeeded in academics leading to careers in whatever had they only gotten the chance or made different decisions. It is arrogant and narrow-minded to think every blue collar person is unintelligent. Dad watched and learned constantly, and he was blessed with a lot of good common sense. He could look at a mechanical problem and think through a way to a proper solution. I know guys who've spent more than half their lives in school who can't do that. He worked with architects and engineers all of the time and once they got to know him, they came to respect him so much that they ran ideas past him. It was amazing to me how often Dad would be called to the Architect's office to consult on jobs and look at prepared blueprints, and I would listen to him pointing out changes that needed to be made in order for the job to work, be easier to fabricate, or easier to install. "That won't work. Look here ..." and he'd point out on their drawings where their folly lay on a daily basis. Unlike them, he was not an educated Architect or Engineer, or a theorist. He was a doer, and doers know that if something isn't done right, something's going to come crashing down. I knew that Dad understood how to fix almost anything; he was known for that, especially at the summer cottage. However, I never really appreciated his true smarts until I was working for their company architect one summer as a then engineering student. On a regular basis, this architect would bring his drawings to Dad for his opinion and make modifications based on his input. This sort of corrected a lot of perceptions I had, as it thoroughly set me back to imagine an architect regularly consulting with someone who didn't complete high school. Marcel admired that as much as I did and so he bonded to him to try to learn everything the old man knew.

Marcel had no problem with what I was doing in searching for my birthparents, yet when I asked, at the time he showed no interest in doing the same for himself. He was immediately hung up on the issue of it appearing disloyal to Mom and Dad. I assured him, as did Mom, that no such a thing could ever be true, yet the issue remained for him. I respected his right to feel that way. All we adoptees have our own choices to make. There is no right or wrong, ever. It simply comes down to choices you make based on the cards dealt you, and the questions you find needing answered. Ultimately, though, once Marcel saw what I went through and how it was turning out so positively, a few years later he started his own search as well. His results are still a work in process as I understand. As he married to a lady that already had children, his life was exponentially busier than mine on the home front! They also had a child together, Josh, who is an amazing spirit.

Soon, Ruth and I were exchanging letters and phone calls with regularity. I was in Toronto and she was living in Des Moines, but we began to speak of somehow visiting one another so we could finally meet face-to-face.

CHAPTER SIX

E PLURIBUS UNUM

"A ring is a halo on your finger."

Doug Coupland

In some of our first calls in the early 90s, Ruth told me about her new (or newer) husband, Bill Lyman. He was ill at the time – cancer – which would stand in the way of our getting together, since she was charged with his care and had her hands full. I understood completely. After all, the big "get" was finding my birth mother. Meeting her in person would be an added bonus, but at least the bigger obstacle was out of the way; I had found her. I now knew who I was.

Bill Lyman was aging and now hospitalized, and Ruth was visiting him every single day in the hospital. She came across to me as someone very loyal and very dedicated to her man. A little eccentric in that regard, too. While the hospital provided good enough care for her man, there were things that simply would not suffice for her as she visited him daily. The idea of Bill's sheets being washed along with all the other sheets in the hospital just did not strike her as right. Call it OCD, call it whatever, but Ruth insisted her Bill sleep on his own soft sheets rather than those rough industrial hospital sheets, and would bring them home daily to clean herself rather than let the hospital clean them. No orderlies stripped or made Bill's bed. That was Ruth's job. She brought in a new clean set of sheets, removed his old ones, took those home to launder, then came back the next day, put a clean set on and took away the old. The hospital had never seen anything before quite like it, but it seemed harmless, since she was saving them time and energy. Bill must have obviously been pleased. Hospital stays are such impersonal affairs. It must have been nice to feel he was almost in his own bed, being catered to by his own wife.

Bill died shortly after my finding Ruth, and I had not the chance to meet him. A bit ironic that I found her just as she was losing another.

It made her more available to me, but it obviously pained Ruth to have lost two husbands now. I felt for her, despite never yet having met her face-to-face yet at that time. On the other hand, Bill's illness had been long and his demise came as no surprise to Ruth or to anyone else for that matter. Still, death is tough.

Ruth sold Bill's home and moved into an adult community efficiency apartment which she and I had discussed. She was getting up in age and it made sense for her to simplify. Her world was more compacted that way, and help, if needed, was close at hand, unlike living in a normal-sized house with land all around it, all by her lonesome. The balance of the proceeds from the sale of Bill's home was expected to carry her through monetarily, since she was "trading down" so to speak. This was at least the perspective I was given at the time, as I was not managing her finances. Hell, we had just contacted each other only a couple months prior, and I hadn't even met her physically yet.

As she was starting to move, Ruth came across a few of Harter's personal things which she had in storage. It had to have been a unique time to come across them. With Bill on the scene, she had to have been somewhat torn, not wanting to appear unfaithful in spirit to her new husband. But now, all alone, and with me, her son, Harter's son, in the picture, the discovery took on a whole different modality. The one thing she came across and sent to me as a gift that first year was some of Harter's Army Air Corp (AAC) personal belongings from World War II. I was completely mesmerized when I saw 2 rings from the war that he wore since entering the AAC, once seemed Army issue, and the other appeared to be a more custom made version of the same, slightly fancier with gold inserts as well as the standard Sterling Silver. I immediately put the custom one on. It fit. I subsequently hadn't taken if off for approximately 17 years. It was a large ring with the Army insignia on each side and the AAC insignia on the face – a propeller intersecting a set of wings. It would be my first and most likely the best link I would ever have to the man who gave me life. Staring at it, I thought of my childhood days, building all those model airplanes, dreaming of someday being a pilot in the armed forces. I thought of the B17 model planes that I had so meticulously built. And now here I was, wearing the ring of an airman; my father's ring, a ring he had earned from having indeed flown these many missions for his country during a time of war. I later found out more details of his service, in that he had flown in over 35 harrowing missions in a B17 Flying Fortress, stationed out of Lavenham England in WWII. It was quite emotional, when I thought back of where my young imagination had often taken me during those model plane building years, completely unaware that that the very visions of my minds eye were actually played out by my father. This speaks to that issue of closure and of the thread of life we all have with those we are related to by blood. Where did my wanderlust for air travel come from? Now I knew. I was perhaps channeling my father, Harter. It was in my genes. Oh how I wished I had the perfect vision required to have been able to fly, but alas, that was not to be. But the desire, that was always there. It came from him.

The other ring was a more standard Army issue, with the same 'winged prop' on the face, but it was entirely made of sterling silver. It also had around the peripheral of the top face the letters "E Pluribus Unum". I later found out this was latin for "Out of many, One", which was an Army motto and one of the nations mottos at the time of the United States seal's creation. In 2011, when my half brother got cancer, I sent the custom ring to him, and I started wearing the standard issue one instead. I felt my half brother, who was raised by Harter and his first wife Peggy, deserved to have that more than I.

My mother and I began to speak and write with greater frequency. It was nice to see things in her own handwriting. I know that sounds strange, but it was something tangible, something I could hold onto. Unlike typing (curse you, Internet!), this was unquestionably touched by her and was an extension of her – the ink, the paper, even the envelope she licked. Every letter became a keepsake. Another cherished thread of life for me.

CHAPTER SEVEN

MEETING MOTHER AND BROTHER

"Gather ye rose-buds while ye may; Old Time is still a-flying; And this same flower that smiles today, Tomorrow will be dying."

Robert Herrick

The summer of 1994, I had made plans to finally come and see Ruth in Des Moines, just before fall. Earlier in the season, I had my cottage in New Brunswick and I was committed to using it and seeing my "real" family, those who had been with me my entire life, as well as old friends and acquaintances which was then, and is now my yearly ritual – one I look forward to more than anything else throughout the year.

It was around this time that Ruth mentioned another family member that I should know about. This was someone she had not brought up when we first discovered each other—my half brother, Stephen Wilband, the boy who had been raised by Agnes in Saint John. My correspondence with Ruth was not such that every single detail of her life came pouring out all at once, which also represented Ruth's character as well– always playing her cards a little close the chest, so to speak. A lot of very, very important things took months and months to appear in our discussions. Cynically, realistically, I look back now and realize some details were slow to come out due to both her private nature as well as, perhaps, some embarrassment. She had not exactly lived the life of a nun, you could say. A kid here, another there; one with this guy, another with another guy. I imagine were I in the same boat, I wouldn't have blurted it all out at once, either. But the existence of more siblings, albeit half-siblings, excited me. These, too, were my blood, connections to my thread of life. If they were alive, I wanted to see them, meet them, look into their eyes and see what I saw of myself, if anything at all. For me, this had another special meaning, since my birth father had passed without me meeting him. This represented an opportunity to see myself in the eyes of another man, and in doing so perhaps see a glimpse of myself. In a way, it could help me get to know a little better what I look like, however odd that may sound.

When we look in the mirror, we sometimes see what we want to see. We may be forty pounds overweight and say, "Man, you're looking good," because that's what we're used to. We'd have to gain perhaps another forty pounds before we'd think, "Hmmm … gotta hit the gym." Yet on others, those first forty additional pounds would make us go, "Yeah, that guy's a little chubby."

Weight is just one of the more basic components. Outside of height, weight, and hair, we adoptees often have a hard time describing ourselves to others. Non-adopted people very often take for granted the very way they look. With family, they get impressions as to how they will eventually look, or how their parents may have looked when they were younger. They share facial expressions that are similar to their parents. They see themselves in their parents, aunts, uncles, and grandparents. In their mirror, they subconsciously know whose eyes, whose ears, whose nose, and whose features are looking back at them. Without really thinking much about it consciously, there is an innate self awareness confidence or grounding in who you are when you know and 'see' images of where you come from. I would argue most who were raised by their birth parents never really think about this in any meaningful way. But I had gone through most of my life having never 'felt' that in any way as I looked in the mirror. I had no base reference to ground me in 'who I looked like', and as such, often left me wondering if I was missing something that those who knew their birth parents. Now I wanted to soak all this in for myself.

I heard the whole Stephen story, about how he was raised in New Brunswick by Agnes. And although it took months for this to be brought to my attention, Blake, who had been dead for years by this time, was a topic that had *not* yet even come up at this point in my genealogical discovery. I knew nothing of him. But Stephen was around and alive and well, and so I wanted to see him, if I could; if it would be all right.

What I later found out behind the scenes was that Ruth had also held back information regarding *me* to *Stephen as well*, and when he finally found out, he was none too pleased, just as had happened regarding Blake, his other half-brother, whom he also had not known about for most of his life. This, I would later learn about from Nancy. First off, Stephen did not know that his birth mother, Ruth, had another child in addition to Blake– me – at all. He did not know she had ever put a child up for adoption. Thus, when he finally was hit with all this, it was in its totality: There was another kid, Ruth had put it up for adoption, and now he had found her … and that "he" was me.

I suppose the fear was that I would visit Ruth in Des Moines and either Stephen might make a surprise trip out there, or Ruth might simply slip and say something, or else someone else might make a similar slip. Nonetheless, in order to get in front of the story, it seemed time to alert Stephen to my existence. Once that was done, Ruth felt more comfortable informing *me and* him. Of course, I was a lot more low-maintenance about the whole thing. I could care less if I had a hundred siblings. I would have actually been overjoyed.

Again, all this was being piecemealed out to me, by and by, and much of the full scope of the story only became apparent to me years later. For example, it was only later that I found out part of the reason for Stephen's pique was that he was also rather late in learning about Blake being his half-brother as well. Fool me once, shame on you; fool me twice, shame on me. For Stephen, this was "brother surprise number two," and I can fully understand how he had every right to be perturbed. Hell, in his shoes I would have felt likewise. I did not, however, find out about his little tiff with Ruth regarding my existence until much later.

That's one of the things with this sort of journey for an adoptee. You want to know everything. You think it is your right to know – and it is. BUT … there are other lives involved. And the birth parents are only two of those lives. Everyone's life is intertwined with countless others. And yes, we all have a right to our privacy. Very few people I know make a point of clearing out their entire skeleton-filled closets to every person they know, and those who do suffer from a chronic case of "TMI" – Too Much Information. On the other hand, certain secrets, such as paternity and the like, when they do find their way back to our doorsteps, can cause life to get sticky in a lot of ways. Ruth seemed overcome with joy that she had found me, but still, there were complications. My mere existence was a complication. I didn't mean it to be, but still and all, it was. It hurt Stephen, and I can relate to what he must have been feeling. I only wish there was something I could have done about it. It probably also threw her current husband for a loop, but perhaps less so. When people meet and marry at a later age, each brings along a trunk full of personal baggage. There are the embarrassments of youth, the embarrassments of poor decisions made along life's way, and then there are simply the components we all accrue along the way. For Ruth, I was all three.

An acute part of how Stephen felt about me was that he and I had grown up in the same city. Hell, we might have even met each other sometime. We may have passed each other on the street. Who knows? It might not have hurt quite as much had I grown up in Phoenix, Arizona or Toledo, Ohio, but no, we both grew up in Saint John. It pissed him off and I understood. As I said, though, at the time *I* heard of *him*, it was like another belated Christmas present to open. Oh boy, a sibling! Another person who might look like me and talk like me and think like me. I couldn't wait to meet him. I mean, on my end, what did I have to lose?

I asked Ruth for Stephen's contact information. She was hesitant at first. Instead, she promised to be the go-between as he and I attempted communication, or shall I say, as *I* attempted to connect with *him*. According to Ruth, Stephen, when presented with the opportunity was quite responsive and did want to meet me. That made me feel good. I guess once the tempers died, he realized that none of this was truly my fault. I mean, I had done nothing wrong. All I did was try to find out who I was. I suppose he figured he could relate to my position and thought that, were the roles reversed, he would have done the same things I did. I wasn't trying to barge into this other family's life like a drunken stock car racer driving into the crowded stands.

Since he was still up in Saint John and I was coming up to the family cottage in the early part of the summer, we made arrangements, brokered through Ruth, to meet. It felt a bit odd to plan a meeting with Stephen before actually having physically met my birth mother Ruth, which would be later in the fall; however this was the way the cards fell since I was already heading up the cottage and would be near Saint John. He had a weekend fishing trip planned with a friend of his who was getting married. The friend was bringing along two of his children. I suppose it was to be your classic "boys' weekend," albeit a very wholesome one.

I was to arrive on a Friday of that very weekend to set up my cottage, and then I said I would drive into Saint John on Monday to meet up with him. By this time, Ruth had given each of us the other's phone number. We still had not yet directly communicated, but still and all, we had a date to meet. When I arrived on Friday, I discussed the situation with an old friend, Scotty M. I told Scotty that I was to meet Stephen following the long week-end fishing trip he was on, and asked for his advice if perhaps I should at least call Stephen prior. Scotty said I should try, but in the end I decided I didn't want to disrupt what Stephen already had planned – as I'm sure the situation was already a bit disruptive as it was, so I didn't call Stephen that Friday evening.

I was excited. I had not yet met my mother in person; I had not yet met anyone related to me by blood. Stephen was to be the first. This was a milestone.

When I had seen pictures of Ruth, I have to admit, I was a little disappointed. Not at all in the way she looked, but rather in my inability to see myself in her initially. I will emphasize "initially," as I suppose I had in my mind's eye seeing an obvious resemblance once I saw her. It took a little time for me see how obvious some traits, in fact, were. As she agreed, I was the spitting image of my father, Harter, but to me, I did not seem to favor her much at all. Later, certain resemblances became more apparent to me. On the other hand, I had not yet seen any pictures of Stephen, so I hoped, perhaps, that once I saw him I would see more of a resemblance there; *something* from the Wilband side of the family. Besides, pictures are only one part of the whole enchilada. There would be mannerisms and so forth. I could get none of that from the pictures I had now of Ruth and Harter. Also, Stephen and I were of the same generation. Sometimes I think it can be hard seeing family resemblances between generations. Ruth was so much older than me.

I was still with Kira at this time. She accompanied me to the cottage and we also had Kira's sister and her husband with us as well on that trip. We also had other friends from the area who were scheduled to come visit with us up at the cottage, so even without Stephen we had a nice-sized crew and we were quite looking forward to some good times with good people. The Stephen thing would just be icing on the cake, and certainly add more discussion for around the bon-fires beside the water in front of the cottage.

On visits to the summer home, although it sat on ocean front property, we'd also hit the local sandy beach near the cottage most days as that was where more people gathered in groups, as well as at a much larger beach called Parlee Beach about ten minutes drive away in Shediac – the self-proclaimed "Lobster Capital of the World!" The cottage days were always some of my favorite days of all time.

On Sunday, the day before I was to meet Stephen, we were all out at the bigger beach ten minutes away. We did not have cell phones back then yet; in fact, we did not even have a landline in my cottage, as I was only there a couple weeks a year. It was rustic and we liked it that way. It was a place to escape technology, not be plugged into it as we were all the other days of the year.

Once we unloaded, one of my neighbors and childhood friends, Maria, wandered over to see me. She looked a little hesitant, which was not her style, as we knew each other very well and I was good friends with her then husband, and also a best friend of her brother Danny. She was kinda like sister in many ways. We certainly fought enough as kids to be! So it was odd to see her acting tentatively.

She asked if I would come outside and take a little stroll with her. I was amicable, but it seemed odd at first.

Once we had gotten a few steps away from the others onto the dirt road in front of the cottage, she said, "Mike, your mom called." Maria and her family had a phone, as they spent far more time in their cottage than we did in ours throughout the year, as their main home was only 30 minutes away. Thus, in case of emergency, we gave people Maria's parent's cottage number in order to reach us, and we also used her phone for outgoing emergency calls. To this day, we still don't have a landline hooked up to our cottage and we still receive calls at Maria's on occasion. Since it was a real hassle to inconvenience these people over just a trifle, if my mom was calling, it was probably something serious.

Maria looked at my face and saw there was no sense of recognition of what she might be about to say. This made neither one of us happy, since it appeared it was to fall upon her shoulders to give me some unpleasant news I most likely did not want to hear. Maria, by the way, along with her brother Danny, were also adopted (small world), and I had told her on the by and by about my search for Ruth and Harter and all, so she also knew all about how I was supposed to meet Stephen, my half-brother, following this particular weekend. It wasn't like I was going around bragging to the whole world about all this stuff at that time. I'm a somewhat private guy, but I think it's always best for one's mental health to have some people around you with which to share various things, and Maria was a good port in the storm to discuss adoption matters.

Maria continued. "Stephen, your half-brother, drowned yesterday."

I looked at her strangely. "What are you talking about? I'm here to see Stephen, and going to see him tomorrow in Saint John," I said, incredulously.

Maria looked down at the ground and then back up at my face as she continued her tale. Apparently Stephen had gone on that fishing trip, as he said he would. He was with another man, whom was identified as a cousin, although it turned out to be just a friend, as I'd been led to believe from the outset. And there were the two young children of this friend along as well – around ages four and seven. Young kids, very young.

In some detail I only found out of much later, apparently while playing on the riverside, the younger of the kids slipped into the river. The adults were upstream a bit fishing from the shore and the kids were down a ways. The kids had been warned to not get too close to the water. They had been standing on a steep bank overlooking the river – not a cliff, but a bank a few feet off the water. Somehow, the younger slipped into the water. The older child, who was still too young to be of much assistance, screamed for help and then jumped into the water on impulse, probably not the best for a youngster. Now, instead of one kid being imperiled, there were two.

Stephen happened to be closer to them on the riverside than the boys' father. He sprinted down the shoreline towards them just after the older boy jumped in, which was fortuitous, since he was able to see exactly where the boy entered the water. When Stephen got there he, too, jumped into the water, and began swimming toward the two children. By the time Stephen had reached them, they were together, the older one having gotten to the younger and grabbed a hold of him. "I'm okay, Stevie," the older child assured him, apparently feeling in control in the currents and maintaining well. The younger one, though, needed assistance getting back to shore, so Stephen left the older one and took the younger child with him, swimming back towards the embankment.

By this time, the boys' father had just reached the shoreline where all three had gone into the drink, as Stephen was able to pass the little boy up to his father and to safety. Stephen then immediately turned around and began paddling back to where the older child had been left treading water. He repeated his actions, reaching and latching on as he began swimming him back to where his father eagerly awaited them both. Again, Stephen handed the second child up the steep bank to his awaiting father. The father turned his back on the water while he sat his child on the grass atop the embankment. When he turned back around to see his friend, Stephen, Stephen was suddenly gone.

Stephen's friend likely panicked a bit. He looked up and down the river as much as was possible without leaving his children, who were tired, wet, and shaken up. He saw nothing. No Stephen. He had been there only a couple seconds earlier, and now he was gone.

Eventually, the friend went for help and came back with some emergency services people. A couple hours went by. Finally, Stephen was found dead, as he was fished out of the river. No one knew exactly what happened. Had the current taken him? Had he accidentally been kicked by in the stomach or groin one of the children during the rescue? Had he just become exhausted by the stress and strain of running and doing all that swimming in order to save the two young boys? Had he simply cramped from sprinting along a river and then swimming twice out into the river and back? Had heaven decided this was an even trade? No one knew. The result, though, was the same. Stephen died heroically saving the two children of his friend.

That night, the local newspaper gave brief coverage to the story. The papers had sanitized the tale somewhat. Apparently, the family of the children did not want the entire tale told, worried that the little children might read it someday and feel guilty for having contributed somehow to this man's death, so there was no mention of Stephen saving anyone. Apparently the older one asked if they caused "Uncle Stevie" to die. The family made a choice to request suppression of the details to the paper so as to not further press that impression on the children. It just said that he was swimming in the river and after the second pass across the river something happened and he was carried away and drowned. Nonetheless, the older child remembered the whole episode rather vividly and had to go into counseling.

It was through the news that my mother – my "real" or adoptive mother, not Ruth – had heard the story and tried to reach out to me up at the cottage. None of the Wilbands tried to contact me as they dealt with the tragedy themselves. I don't blame them. They all had to have been in too much shock. Stephen was in the prime of his life. He was far too young to die, and it had all been so sudden and without warning.

I was utterly devastated. I didn't know what to think. So close. So damn close. In less than 24 hours I was going to meet my half-brother, the first time in my life I was to meet a blood relative and possibly see myself in the eyes of a relative for the first time and now this. I could not have dreamt up anything crazier if I was trying to write a Hollywood movie.

The entire rest of the night I was in a complete haze. It was one of those times when I just couldn't sit still, even though I had no idea what I could do. I turned to Kira and told her that she would be fine with her sister and her brother-in-law, but I simply could not just hang out and socialize, as we tended to do on those summer evenings up at the cottage. I mean, we had no electronics; there was nothing really to do but sit around and shoot the breeze, which normally I would have enjoyed, but not tonight. I told her I wanted to drive into town – Saint John – and figure out my next move from there. She didn't hold me back.

I was on vacation, so I hadn't packed anything formal to wear; nothing like a suit or anything like that, as one typically doesn't expect to attend a funeral on their vacation. I knew there would be a funeral and I knew Stephen would be waked as well. My need to be there superseded my wardrobe. I just threw on the nicest "formal wear" I had: a pair of khaki shorts and the cleanest polo shirt I'd brought with me. I assumed it would be an open casket, although I didn't know for sure, and if I didn't show up, I would miss out on my one and only time to look at the face of my half-brother, Stephen.

They waked Stephen very quickly. I know, sometimes a funeral takes almost an entire week to arrange and do, but in his case, he was being shown fairly fast. I had no idea why, but it was not for me to question. By the time I got to Saint John, there was only one hour left before the wake would be over that evening. I knew which funeral home he would be at; my mother relayed all the information to Maria, along with the hours and the wake schedule.

I didn't have time to go home to visit my mom or anything like that. All I had time for was to drive immediately to the funeral home. I hadn't thought much of this out frankly. It only vaguely occurred to me there would be lots of Wilbands there and that I would have heard of a lot of them from my recent correspondence with Ruth, who I had also not physically met face to face yet either. That was scheduled to occur later on at the end of the summer. Normally, meeting the new relatives would have excited and elated me, but due to the situation, all I felt was a pressing depression for having come so close to meeting Stephen and then having that rug pulled out from under me.

The funeral home where the wake was held was in one of the older, row house-type structures in old Saint John. It had been around forever. Inside, there were a couple viewing rooms so they could accommodate more than one funeral at a time. When I arrived, yet another bizarre surprise awaited me. As would be the usual protocol, I was greeted at the door by the funeral director, who would act almost as a maitre d', making sure folks got to the correct family room where the body would be displayed. However this greeting was not so typical, by any measure. Lo and behold, as I entered the funeral home I was awakened from my gloom slightly by a familiar voice. "Mike!" The voice belonged to a woman and she sounded not only familiar, but sounded glad to see me; in fact, it seemed initially like she may have felt I was possibly there to see *her*, rather than to attend to some mourning. I looked up and the funeral director representative was Nancy, an old high school crush of mine. We had dated briefly on and off through a couple years of school. Certainly, I wasn't dressed as if I were coming to pay respects, as being on a summer vacation doesn't usually include packing a black suit, no the best outfit I had in my suitcase was more akin to Sunday BBQ attire. No wonder she may have thought I was there to see her. I had no idea she even worked at a funeral home, let alone this one. I had so lost track of her I didn't even know what her chosen field was. I had moved away immediately after high school, so there were many friends and classmates who I had not followed their careers – only my closest friends and I stayed tight in that respect. Apparently the business connection emanated from someone in her family. Perhaps I should have known that. Goes to show how attentive a high school boy is, I suppose. Still, it was odd. How many kids do you know growing up that you think, "Geez, I bet she'd make a nice funeral director"? I mean, it's kind of like going into the priesthood. Not many kids do it or even talk about it, but still, a few do, obviously. Oddly enough, and old cottage friend of mine who owns the property across from ours, Sandra A, has a spouse named Marc M who is actually a funeral director himself. So I guess not as rare a profession as I once thought – and for sure a profession that will never go obsolete !

"What are you doing here?" Again, the tone appeared as if I was paying her a surprise visit. Since she had stayed in our hometown and since funeral directors know *everybody*, she must have done a quick mental inventory and could not for the life of her connect me to any of the deceased who were there that evening.

"I'm here to see my brother." That knocked her back on her heels. She knew I had a brother Marcel, and she was darn sure *he* certainly wasn't dead and lying in her care that evening, so she was completely flummoxed. Me, I was still in a complete haze. I couldn't lie, make stuff up, or be evasive in any way for the life of me. The blues will do that to you. They're a great truth serum.

I quickly and without real explanation told her I was there to see 'another' brother Stephen Wilband, that it was a bit complicated and could she point me in the right direction. She did, but it was obvious she wanted more information. I added, if she would be so kind, could I please catch up with her once I had gone in to pay my respects. She agreed, seeing the distress and far-away look on my face. As a funeral director, she must have been used to things like this; the moods of mourning and loss. Her job was to be understanding, and understanding she was. I can only imagine the things she has seen in this profession, and professional she was in dealing with me that day.

I don't know what I expected. Maybe in my own mind I imagined I would walk in and it would be just me and the casket. But no, there was a room full of people. There were a lot of Wilbands in general, since many of them remained in Saint John, so there was quite a contingent there. And since Stephen himself had stayed in the area, I'm sure he had many friends and acquaintances there to pay their respects.

As I walked into the room, wearing my vacation funeral home best Khaki shorts, things started to slow down a bit as if watching a slightly reduced speed black and white film. The number of people there overwhelmed me a little as they became blurred somewhat as I scanned for a casket. Not exactly the vision I had of meeting my first blood relative face to face. This would not be some private moment for me and him, but a moment I would have to share with a whole lot of others. I wasn't happy about that, but it was what it was and I just had to roll with it. This was however the same timeframe we had formally agreed to meet, so logistically we were on schedule in an ironic sense. Everyone else was dressed nicely, the men in suits, the women in dresses, and here I was looking like I was ready for my tee time at the local public golf course. I stuck out like a parrot in a punch bowl.

Had I thought it out, I might have first tried to mingle around, to find out who was there and to introduce myself so I could connect to the various members of my birth family, but I couldn't wrap my head around that in such a short amount of time. Instead, I instinctively figured it would be best if I just walked up to the casket and did my thing there. Luckily, despite there being so many people at the time, most of them had already done the respects deed and were now just mingling about. Scanning quickly across the now blurred faces in search of the target, I spotted the casket with no one kneeling at it. I then sort of went into auto-pilot. I had a clear shot and so I took it. I made my way straight up to the casket and knelt down. Here I was, trying to get to know Stephen in only a few seconds time. How strange and how sad that it was to be a one-way communication.

I just stared at him for awhile. I looked at his face. He had normally worn a mustache, or so I'd been told. I later found out that the funeral parlor had given him a clean shave, assuming his three day stubble, along with the mustache, was simply the product of a few days fishing, but in actuality, they represented how he would regularly appear. I'm sure things like that happen all the time at funeral parlors, unfortunately. His family was a bit upset, since it was not how he normally looked, but what did I know? For me, it was the first and last time I would lay eyes on my biological brother.

I can't say I saw any overwhelming resemblance between us at that time, other than a full head of hair. Still, even if I did, I don't know if I could have properly processed it right there and then. I later was told that if we resembled each other at all, it was in the form of our mannerisms, and since he was dead, there was no way I was going to be able to see that. Apparently, I can have a bit of a naturally stern look about me, and that seemed to be a Wilband trait that Ruth, Stephen, and I shared. It's not that I *am* a stern person; it's more that when I am concentrating on something, I tend to appear stern. So be it. At least now I know where I got it from. I can still remember being a little kid, even watching something like The Flintstones on TV, and my mother saying, "Why are you so upset?" In actuality I wasn't upset at all. I was just being me, and when I watched TV, that was the expression on my face. Likely not something a birth parent would mistake as a child's natural mannerisms.

When I would eventually collect pictures of Stephen from Ruth, I began to see that he didn't even resemble Ruth all that much. He must have taken more after his own father, who was not *my* biological father. He was shorter than me and had much darker hair and skin, among other things.

I was riding on emotion as I knelt there. I was a bit lost in the many thoughts rushing through my mind, and then began to realize I'd been kneeling there a little longer than I should have and so I said a little prayer after "getting to know him," and got back to my feet. When I stood up, I felt completely out of place. It was a strange, self-conscious feeling. Things again were almost going in slow motion as I stood, feeling the eyes of a room full of people boring through the back of my head. I felt like I had to bolt, to get out of there as quickly as possible. I don't know why. I guess I felt like a party crasher who wanted to leave before I was asked to leave; I don't know. It was unrealistic for me to feel that way, but as I said, I was feeling more than thinking, and so I acted on whatever feelings I was having at the time.

When I turned to face the rest of the room, it felt like everyone there was staring at me, like I had just did something wrong. It was pure paranoia, I'm sure of it, but it felt bad and it made me want to leave even faster. Some of them, indeed, knew Stephen was supposed to meet his long lost half-brother that very day, and maybe they put two and two together; I don't know.

I made a beeline for the door. What took only seconds to reach the door seemed like minutes as thoughts continued to pour through my head, and again faces blurred as I moved towards my goal like a rushing stream of water pouring over anything in its way. Just before I reached it, the dumbest, most obvious thing in the world hit me like a hammer. There must be someone in this room, someone very important, whom I had not met yet in person. Someone was there who was not supposed to be in New Brunswick this week, or anywhere near for that matter. My mother. *Our* mother. Ruth. Ruth had to have been there. I don't know why it took me until that very moment to figure that one out, but I was three-quarters of the way out of the room before it occurred to me. I had been so consumed in the shock of the event, it hadn't even dawned on me to call her. My mother, *who again I had not yet met* in person actually, as that was planned for later the following month in Des Moines, had to have been in that very room at the very same moment as I. The person I'd spent years wondering about was only a few feet away from me; I just knew it, I felt it. As she wasn't *supposed* to be in

Canada at that time, but since her son had just died, of course she would be there. After years of searching, not quite the environment I would ever have imagined in my wildest dark dreams where I would meet my birth mother, in a funeral parlor after just meeting my deceased brother.

What should I do? At that very moment the hazy feeling intensified further, as did the slowed motion of everything around me. A lot of it had to do with how I had handled the entire thing. I hadn't gotten on the phone and talked any of this out with my mother. I hadn't let Kira in and shared my feelings with her, either. I just put blinders on and kept my own counsel; a mistake I had made many times in the past, wanting to "handle it on my own." Had I talked it through with someone else who cared about me, all of these things would have been more apparent to me. The time seemed to rush so fast as I handled it in a complete haze, that the obvious did not occur to me. Instead, I was acting and feeling a little lost as needed to make a decision to act on, while in full motion towards the door.

My pace slowed only slightly. I felt I should take a quick glance sideways and try to focus a bit on faces as I approached the door to exit the room. Again, it felt like everyone there had eyes burning through me. I didn't know how to deal with that, already feeling like a party crasher. Part of me wanted to double back and wade back into the crowd to see who these people were, but the physical part of me felt like I had already hurdled myself out of a plane, heading for that door and unable to stop.

I was just about to the door opening when almost instinctively I looked to my right and paused ever so noticeably, again almost like in slow motion. I saw a cluster of people that seemed to move towards me, yet were separating at the same time, like a flower rising toward the sun while blossoming. There, blocked at first by the crowd but now appearing at the center of the throng, was my mother, Ruth.

She stared at me like she saw a ghost. We needed no introduction. We had exchanged photographs over the past few months. I knew it was her and she knew it was me. We spoke volumes with only our eyes in what was only seconds. Still, I remained in motion towards the door, although I had slowed incredibly. Instinctively and instantly as I entered the door threshold I took my right hand, made the thumb and little finger symbol, and brought it up to my ear in the universal "telephone" sign and mouthed the words, "I'll call you." With that I continued my motion and slipped out the door of the parlor room.

Was it the right thing to do? I don't know. Probably not. I just knew how I felt in those realization seconds, and how I felt was that this was just not the time or the place to have a first union with my birth mother. This day was about Stephen Wilband. He died, and died heroically, saving two little kids who might have drowned without him. He deserved his due. Everyone was there for him, to remember him. How crass it would have been to make this day about me, the interloper, the party-crasher, invading Stephen's world and the world of the entire Wilband family, introducing new and undue additional emotion to that room. I felt at peace with how I stepped aside out of courtesy to another.

Truth was I also couldn't wait to get out of the building. I completely forgot about my brief high school "girlfriend," if I could call her that, whom I had promised to chat with once I was on my way out. I was too lost in thought. Catching up with an old friend was the last thing on my mind at that time, unfortunately. I would perhaps later come back to apologize and explain another time.

The actual funeral was the next day. I spent the night at my parents' house. I had every intention of going to the church for the funeral. I jumped in the car and drove over to the church parking lot, but once I arrived, at the last minute I decided to stay in the car during the service. Again, I felt out of place, but not just in a shy way. Again, I felt my presence there would be wrong. I wanted to see Stephen for selfish reasons, although I don't believe I could be blamed for that. Were the roles reversed, I imagine he would have done the same thing in trying to still connect with me. I know he wanted to meet me, to see me, to figure out more about himself by learning more about me. Just looking at a corpse was rather lackluster, but still, I believe he would have made a similar effort were the roles reversed. I was also doing it out of respect for the dead. We do these things in life; it's part of our responsibility to each other. But I hesitated again regarding the aspect of drawing too much attention away from Stephen and onto myself. I stayed in the car.

Time dragged on. I was not bored. I thought. I thought about everything. I reflected back upon seeing my birth mother for the first time, although we spoke not a word to one another. Still, I saw her and she saw me. She was real. With phone calls and letters, there is still an unreal element about it all. But when I saw her, I knew it was her. I knew she was real and she was really my mother, which is a mindblower for an adoptee at that moment. I had finally found her. However, it is very unlikely that people who search for their birth parents end up seeing one for first time in a funeral parlor, at the wake of another son. It was very surreal for me.

The church doors opened up and people in black came out and began filing into their cars. When they turned on their motors, I turned mine on as well. I hadn't a plan, but I knew I wanted to still somehow be a part of what was happening, even if no one else knew it but me.

I hung back, but remained close enough to see where they were headed. They turned onto Loch Lomond Road in East Saint John, a place I was quite familiar with. My mother's sister Ermyn and husband Buster were buried in the same cemetery they were heading for, and eventually would also be my father who raised me, along with some other members of our family. I passed the place every time I went to 'the big shopping mall' nearby during childhood.

When I got within eyeshot of the place, I took a left when the entire procession took a right. They were going into the actual cemetery; me, I just wanted to pull over and hang out somewhere nearby until I got a bearing on where in the cemetery the plot might be. On the very opposite side of the road from the cemetery, I found myself in a parking lot for a motorcycle type dealership that was there at the time, I believe, called something like "Toys for Big Boys." From there, I could see across exactly where the other cars were going. Heck, I could actually see specifically where inside the cemetery they were heading, only one row inside the cemetery, and parallel to the main road that I had pulled left off. The crowd gathered on this parallel road facing Stephens plot. From this point, they actually faced me as well across the street. From my vantage point, I could actually stand and watch the actual graveside ceremony, everyone on one side of the plot, and me alone on the other, albeit across the street.

I got out of my car and leaned against a tree, somewhat hidden in the shade. I was far enough away that no one would have thought to look over to see me. I continued to feel in a sort of haze, a little in auto-pilot flowing with the breeze. I also felt a little like a voyeur, feeling like I was Humphry Bogart in a black and white film, with trench coat on with collar pulled up for anonymity. The entire situation seemed to suit my attitude. I was an outsider, and so I chose to remain outside out of respect. This was their moment, but still, I was able to participate and look in on it. If only Stephen and I had connected a day or a week earlier, it might have been different, but that was not to be. Fate is strange that way.

At my parent's home I'd managed to scrounge up a pair of long pants and a nicer shirt, but still, no suit, and certainly no proper black suit like all the other men were wearing. This, too, made me feel out of place and made me feel glad I'd chosen to stay a safe distance away.

With Stephen's plot the second row in, parallel from the road, and everyone situated facing in my direction, I felt a little strange, but again, I was far enough away that I doubt they noticed me underneath the tree. But me, I could see their faces, all of them, although they were tiny and hard to distinguish. It kind of gave me a front row seat to the event.

I couldn't hear anything, but I watched everyone's body language. I suppose if you've been to one funeral, you've been to them all. Nothing unusual, nothing unique. Some folks were more upset than others and needed support. I get that.

The service seemed long, but eventually there was movement and people began heading for their cars. The majority left right away, although a handful lingered on. Still, I remained in exactly the same stance, back against the tree, taking it all in motionlessly. After a time, even the lingerers made their way to their cars and exited. A final couple, younger people, stayed longer that everyone, and then they too started on their way.

Once every car had pulled away, I finally walked across the street. All that remained were two cemetery guys, doing their jobs. I'd never seen their duties before and in a strange way, it was kind of fascinating. During the graveside service, they always lower the casket very slowly, right there in front of the mourners. What I came to see was that once everyone is gone, they at times bring it back up again. Odd. They remove a green carpet material covering the inside walls of the six feet under, they put the casket into a pine frame and lower it back down again. Next, they shovel the dirt into the hole until it forms a mound. Lastly, they take the flowers and arrange them purposefully around and on top of the mound so it looks nice and neat for anyone coming around a day or two after the service.

I stood by and watched all this, time seemed to go very fast, although it took near 30 minutes I expect. The two workers paid me no mind, nor did I try to chat them up. I was so ignored that they just went about talking with each other like any other two guys at any regular job site. One was older and the other younger; they could almost have been a father and a son. One of them mentioned what a big crowd it was that day, the biggest either had seen all summer. I suppose that made sense. It *was* a large crowd. The younger one is when one dies, the larger the crowd it also seems. That, and the old saying about how the weather has such an impact on how many people come to your funeral. You spend your whole life trying to make an impact on the world, and a rainstorm can drive all the people away and it's as if you hadn't a friend in the world. But today was a sunny day and the weather kept no one from attending.

The entire time, I'm just standing there with my hands shoved in my pockets, looking like I had no idea what to do with myself. Honestly,

I didn't even know why I was there. I guess I was just drawn to this place, and felt I needed to be there, like there was a purpose for all of this. Finally, after a half an hour or so, one of the workers noticed me and asked the natural question. "Was a big funeral. So, you know this guy, huh?" referring to the deceased.

I could have said, "Yeah, he's my brother," which I did with Nancy and which would have made them feel this was very natural, but no, I stuck to a more honest truth that was actually the first thing that came to my mind. "No, I didn't know him," I said, and it was true; I didn't. I never knew Stephen Wilband. We shared some DNA, but nothing more than that. We'd made a date to meet, but it was through a third-party and we never even spoke together on the phone. I thought of all the people in the world I knew, all the people I had shared a moment or a word with, and Stephen Wilband wasn't one of them.

After I said it, it struck me how odd my answer must have seemed to these two men, but with the haze I was in, it didn't seem that important. However, putting myself in their place, I'd have thought, "Ok we got a weirdo here watching us bury people. If he didn't know the guy, what the hell is he doing standing here? Is he some sort of ghoul?" I don't know what they thought, but inside I kind of laughed derisively at myself. What did I care what these two guys thought? The past 24 hours, all I had done was ponder what others were thinking of me. That was so unlike me. I'm not a slave to peer pressure, but here I was, trying to tip-toe around the world I surveyed, unsure of myself, afraid of being an unsettling presence. All the while I was conscious of how they seemed to look for an explanation, yet somehow other thoughts continued to take precedent over that lingering thought for me.

They finished their work while I remained. I watched as they put the finishing touches very tastefully, like seasoned gardeners. I thought for a moment they might say something, something as to what the hell was I up to, but they couldn't be bothered. They went on their way. Now I was all alone, just me and Stephen underneath a fresh mound of dirt. My mind had been in a lot of strange places over the past few days, yet none of them was overly emotional. I know that sounds like a contradiction, but it isn't. I was thinking and doing and worrying, but not engaging in a lot of pure emotion. That was, until this very moment. Now, for the first time, I felt a sense of loss, of having had something taken away from me. It was like some sort of cosmic joke. You're about to see a guy, your own brother, for the first time in your life and then he dies a few hours before you are to meet. A young, healthy guy just up and dies. What kind of craziness is that, Lord?

I stayed for another fifteen or twenty minutes after the two cemetery workers left. The haze lifted for the first time at what had just happened—all of it. I didn't quite cry, but I know I felt for the first time a tremendous amount of emotion swell up in me, and shortness of breath, pressure in my throat, and with a furrowed brow I fought off my watering eyes. Sometimes it's not about tears; it's about how you feel deep down inside, and deep down inside I felt like I'd lost something. I felt grief.

I finally walked away and got back into my car. It was a sunny summer day, far too pretty a day for a young man's funeral. It should have been dreary and overcast, but it wasn't. Even the weather seemed to contradict what was going on.

I got back to my parent's house and called Ruth, who I figured correctly was at Agnes's house. Agnes answered the phone. I had never actually spoken with her before and I did not have her number on me, but she was listed in the Saint John phone book, which, of course, my mom had at her house. I spoke to Agnes, explaining to her who I was. She was not taken by surprise. I imagine all the Wilbands knew about me by that point. I asked to speak with Ruth and I told Agnes what I had in mind, in case she was wondering.

Ruth and I made arrangements for me to swing by. I know Ruth had in her mind that I would come in and meet the entire Wilband clan, but that wasn't going to work for me. I said, "Look, first and foremost, I want to officially meet you. You're my mother. I know there's a lot going on over there and I don't want to be a bother or a disruption, but if I could, what I'd like to do is just spend a bit of time with you and you alone, one-on-one. Can we do it that way, and broaden the circle later with the family?" She agreed to my terms. I drove over to Agnes's and Ruth was waiting for me outside. I opened the passenger door to my car and let her in. She stared a moment at me and one hand came up to her face, and her first words were, "You have Stephen's mouth." It seemed an odd thing at the time, but I suppose having just lost a son, it would be heavy on her mind to look for things that would remind her of him, and Ruth, of course, the mother of us both, would know, so I took her word for it. I asked if I could take her somewhere for a drive and she agreed. I could tell she sort of wanted to take me inside and show me off to everyone as a proud mother. I compromised by promising her that when I brought her back, I would go inside and say hello to the others. That seemed to satisfy her.

Ruth said she'd already eaten, so I decided to take her to a coffee shop: Tim Horton's Doughnuts. In Canada, they are about as common as Dunkin Donuts is in the US. Horton was an NHL hockey player and he started a doughnut chain that spread like wildfire. In Canada, there's one on every corner. It seemed an appropriate place to have a cup of coffee and relax.

I don't know how many cups of coffee or how many doughnuts we went through, but we stayed there for hours and hours, just talking about literally everything. This was as I had wanted it, although the specter of the funeral still hung 'round my head from time to time, as I'm sure it did Ruth's. That was the only thing that made this entire reunion so odd. But this chat, it was good, very good.

From Tim Horton's, I drove her to my mom and dad's place. I got out a camera and the very first picture I actually took of my birth mother, I took in front of a tree near the home in which I grew up. Again, how odd, and yet how poignant.

Looking at Ruth, I was amazed at how petite she was. I'm not a small guy and so I guess I was expecting someone a little more substantial. She was very proper and very well-dressed. You could tell she went out of her way to take care of herself. Her hair was grey. When I say she took care of herself, I meant for a woman of her age. I still had a bit of trouble arranging that part of it in my head. I had long expected someone who would be almost the age of an older sister; given what Catholic welfare had told my mom when she adopted me. Instead, Ruth seemed almost like a grandmother to me, a grandmother *of* me. I had trouble getting past that. It made her identity seem at times unreal. She was twelve years older than my *own* mother.

My mom and dad were both working and neither was there. I suppose I could have been more insistent that they try to make an appearance, but it didn't seem right. I know my parents wanted to meet Ruth, most likely to thank her. Were it not for her, they would have never gotten me. I know, some people ask whether my parents felt jealous or anything like that. Far from it. Our relationship was solid and well-established. They supported my search for my birth parents and here I had found one of them, as Harter had already passed.

I then drove Ruth back to Agnes's place. This time I got out. I met her brother; I met Agnes, as well as a slew of other Wilbands. There were probably more there earlier, so I'm kind of glad I got there when I did. In many ways, I wanted to meet them all, but not like this. Some other time, under a far better circumstance. Still, there were a number of them there and they seemed like a tight-knit family. When you go to a family gathering, you can get a feel for things in a very short time. This family was close, which I thought was pretty cool. They were more outgoing than I would have imagined. Ruth, ironically, was one of the least outgoing. She seemed to be the shy one, the reticent one. I can be a bit that way as well at times. It was one of the first things I thought I might have inherited from her, watching her interact with her family. Agnes was an amazing spirit herself. The oldest of the sisters, she came across as "everyone's mother", similar to my mom Joan. A very nice presence.

Everyone was very friendly to me, which I appreciated. I was filled in on various family stories and tales. No one brought up Blake, my other half-brother. He, I would not find out about until another time much later. No one talked about him. I suppose there were still some open wounds about his untimely death as well. The next day, I had dinner with Ruth at a restaurant, where we got to know each other further, and grieved about Stephen's passing together.

From there I went back to my cottage and rejoined Kira and friends, back to what was left of my official vacation. All in all, it was most certainly the strangest vacation of my life. Sometimes even an organized journey can take you places you never planned on arriving.

CHAPTER EIGHT

MY DAD OR OUR DAD ?

"No one remains quite what he was when he recognizes himself."

Thomas Mann

Ruth gave me lots and lots of information on my birth father, Harter, but I wanted to dig even further. I'm a man. The things that interest us may not necessarily always be the things most in the forefront of women's minds. This isn't me being sexist; it just is what it is. Being a detail-oriented engineer also didn't help. For example, I wanted to know every single thing about his military experience. Ruth was not yet in Harter's life when he served during WWII, and while she did know a few things, such as going with him on his later pilgrimages to England and such, many of the details mattered little to her. They may not have even discussed it much when they were together while he was alive. A lot of men don't talk a lot about their war experiences. Often, the guys who talk the most are the ones who did the least! The guys who saw the most action, many of them take those experiences with them to the grave, distraught over the carnage they saw up close and firsthand.

On the Internet, I found a discussion group dedicated to the 487th Bombing Group out of Levenham, England. I left several messages on the online bulletin board there looking for anyone who may have known Harter. Eventually, I had some hits, some people who knew or were related to some people who flew with this contingent. The most helpful contact was a woman whose father flew several missions with Harter. We arranged to chat over the phone and it was quite enlightening.

All along, I'd wanted to go visit Ruth in Des Moines, which had been our original plan for meeting prior to Stephen's untimely death. After Stephen's funeral I eventually followed through with that. It was not only where she lived, but it was Harter Hull's town and always had been. Coming there would give me a better sense of who he was, just as Saint John told a lot about Ruth and me.

By this time, with her second husband gone, Ruth was living in an elder-care residence, a high rise wherein she had an efficiency apartment. It was modest but nice. It was a small place but she managed to cram into it every one of her memories. I could relate to that. When it all comes down, the older we get, the more we cling to things that have an intrinsic value rather than a monetary one. She even rented space in an external storage unit for the overflow.

We'd go out to dinner and she'd take me to all the places she and Harter used to frequent. For her, it was a trip down memory lane. There was no question she loved him and he had been the one true love of her life. For me, every place we went, ever tale she'd tell, just fleshed out those pictures of him I'd seen. It was bringing him to life for me. Seems Harter loved to go out, eat fancy dinners, and smoke an expensive cigar. In other words, he was a classic American hedonistic male, a lover of the good life, and who could fault him for that? He was a classy guy, albeit perhaps a bit dominating at times, from the stories I've heard from Ruth's sisters and his ex-flight crew pal.

Like most Midwesterners, he loved a good steak, and Ruth would take me to all his favorite steak joints, places where the meat was as thick as your fist, hung over the side of the plate, and cost half a week's salary for the average guy. Sitting there across from my mother, I sort of felt like I was channeling Harter, as if for a moment he was deep down inside of me, seeing it all again, except this time through my eyes. You want to talk about eternal life? Children. Children are our eternal life. When we create them, we go on and on forever. Part of him is part of me. I thought about that a lot as I listened to Ruth spin her stories, and thought also of my daughter Alexandra one day taking the baton and moving through even more decades of life, remembering her old man, and even when she wasn't, still carrying on aspects of me for future days to come.

Some adoptees in my situation may have made the pilgrimage to

Des Moines just once, but I did it numerous times. I could afford it and I could manage it with my work and life schedule, so why not? Some adoptees just want to eyeball their birthmother once, ask a few of the basic questions: "Why did you not keep me?" and then turn and go back to life as they had come to know it. Me, I was actually enjoying time spent with my mother. She was an okay gal. Plus, even if she had not been, so long as she still was willing to keep in contact with me, I am of a curious mind. It was not enough for me to run through the list of the first five questions every adoptee has. My list grew and grew. It grew with every moment we spent together. It was less of an inquisition and more of a rambling conversation around a metaphorical campfire or local pub. I'm a good listener. I like to learn. Taking to Ruth, I was learning more and more about myself, in an oblique way. I am half Ruth Wilband and half Harter Hull. Who the heck were these people? I wanted to know.

She was not the most open book, and with a natural "cards close to her chest" demeanor, you had to selectively pick the rabbit hole you wanted to go down. I was conscious of not making it an interview each time we met, so I'd often listen to her tell me about the folks in the home for the elderly where she lived. About the older gentleman giving her extra attention, and how she thought he may want to be her man, but she wasn't interested in him. He was "too rough around the edges" for her. She seemed pretty picky. The stories made me smile inside.

The visits never lasted long. When I was in Iowa with her, I'd act as any good son would, taking Ruth out and running errands for her or with her, providing her with transportation. It's a natural thing for me. I was raised to respect my elders and thus I respect Ruth. It was my natural duty to do so.

During these trips, Ruth was very proud to introduce me around to all the people she knew, especially in the home. She was unabashed. I think a lot of it is the realities of age. Once you reach certain milestones in life, what the heck do you care what people think of who you were and what decisions you made back when you were young? I was never asked to pretend to be anyone other than who I was: Ruth's long lost son whom she put up for adoption many, many years ago. If she was good with that, then so was I. I couldn't have asked for better parents than those that raised me, regardless.

I even came to acquaint myself with the staff at the facility in which she lived, particularly the lady who ran the place. The good thing about that is it gave me a neutral, third-party insight into how Ruth was doing now in her elder years. A lot of older folks don't admit when they are struggling on some level or another, but others around them often know the truth. I made a point of giving my contact information to the lady in charge, telling her that if Ruth ever needed anything or if she was ever in some sort of distress; she was to call me immediately so I could help. Ruth was my mother. This was my duty.

At the start of our relationship, Ruth was, in fact, in good health for her age. She had an inhaler for some sort of respiratory problem, but nothing major. In other words, she was pretty much as healthy as the average person, or so it seemed.

The chronology of all this is that I was still married to Kira. It was the sunset of the good days between us; not that we knew that at the time. It was before she got really sick and started having serious health problems, let alone had had her major brain surgery. Nonetheless, this was still MY thing. It did not demonstrate a coolness between Kira and I; it was just the way we both felt it should be handled. Ruth was *my* mother. *I* should be the one to run out to Des Moines. *I* was the one who needed the private bonding time. I'm sure if I asked Kira to join me in this adventure she would have, but we talked it out and we were both good with the arrangement we had made. The way we both saw it, as it was developing before our eyes, we assumed that eventually she too would meet up with Ruth at some point, and we would all be one big happy family, along with my parents in Saint John.

I had not yet gotten up the nerve to contact Harter's children. I hadn't really discussed them with Ruth yet, but she had informed me that Harter did, indeed, have children with his first wife, Peggy. That weirded me out again, too. I'd come to feel that Harter had no idea I existed and that I'd been his. Now here he was with two children from his first marriage, the only children he did know for sure that he had, and they had been going through life blissfully unaware of my existence. I empathize with these sorts of people. You're a kid. You grow up, you look around your house, you look at your mom and dad and your siblings and you assume, "This is it." This is your nuclear family. There are some cousins and some aunts and uncles, but they're more on the periphery of your life. Imagine, then, your phone ringing one day and some strange voice saying, "Hi, I'm your long lost half-brother. Pleased to meet you!" It's creepy. It's creepy in its own right and it's not fair. Nonetheless, I'm sure it happens to its share of people worldwide. It's far different than with, say, Ruth. Ruth knew she had a child and put it up for adoption. When I came back into her life, it was something she'd always thought might be coming, some day, some way. But Harter's kids? They hadn't a clue. For that reason, I wasn't ready to race out and do it. Ruth had not yet volunteered their contact information, either, but for the time being, I wasn't going to ask for it, at least not yet.

From what I'd heard, Harter's divorce had been a bitter one. I can't say I blame his first wife for feeling betrayed. Truth is, the man did cheat on her and left her for another woman. This had to have been hard on his kids from that marriage, as I would eventually find out. Ruth moving to Iowa couldn't have helped, either. My strolling into the family's life would just be another poke in the eye.

Early on, though, I managed to find and contact Harter's sister in Florida. She, of course, was Harter's blood rather than related by marriage and stood a better chance of being simpatico towards me. Harter's sister lived long enough to have received the bounty of their mother's estate. She also had a husband with a solid career, so she and her family lived rather well. Harter's mother had passed not long before I first connected with Ruth.

I talked to Harter's sister once or twice and she was quite lovely. She sent me some pictures of her and Harter, which I treasured. My favorite picture of all, the one where I could really see him so clearly and could see my resemblance to him, came from her. It was a sepia patina'd picture of Harter with his leather flight bomber jacket on, chest held high and full, posing with a pipe in his mouth. Not sure if he smoked a pipe regularly or if this was simply a standard fly-boy picture where the photographer said "Hold this pipe; it'll make you look more sophisticated." I have that picture framed in my living room and find it looks a lot like me when He is posed in the picture with his arms crossed, and you can see the AAC ring Ruth sent me on his hand. I was around twenty nine years old at that time, so I appreciate greatly his sister sending me that. Shortly after we had connected, though, she passed away, much to my chagrin.

What amazed me, as I came in contact with more and more people associated with my birth family, was that no one treated me shabbily. I imagine in some cases, in theoretical situations such as this, a person might consider someone like me to be some sort of money-hungry interloper. But no, even before I went into my song and dance with these people, I was always welcomed with open arms. Nonetheless, I made it very, very clear why I was reaching out and it sure as hell had nothing to do with trolling for money.

A lot of this had to do with getting in touch with Ruth so early on. Having established some trust and credibility with her regarding my intentions, she would often call ahead on my behalf, introducing me to people and vouching for my character. I appreciated that and it seemed to have worked well. I suppose it also helped that I was well-established in my career and, while I may not have stepped out of a limousine or a private jet, it was clear to most who met me that I could hold my own as a working man and provider.

I spent years on this continued search. Talk to many people who begin tracing their genealogy and they'll tell you it's like that. But this was different. I wasn't chasing the dead as much as I was pursuing the living. Sure, I wished a thousand times I could have begun this entire quest while Harter was still alive, but those who knew him and were related to him were still around, people who knew him first-hand. It wasn't about knowing how long my people had been in North America or anything like that. I didn't know who the hell I really was, and I wasn't going to die without knowing!

I went back time and again to websites that chronicled the adventures of Harter's flight squad and came in contact with more and more people who were related to guys who served with him. It was great. Unlike some people, I actually enjoyed hearing their old war stories.

Eventually, though, it gnawed at me that I had this half-brother and half-sister whom I had never met. Time had passed and I had hidden in plain sight. People associated with other people had come to know there was this Mike guy who was Harter's long lost bastard child, and that he wasn't such a bad egg.

It was around this time that I found the time to search out and get to know someone else in my genealogy. I finally took the plunge and reached out to my half-brother, Harter's son, the son who thought he was Harter's *only* son. By now I'd been to Des Moines a few times to see Ruth. Many of Harter's people were still in that same town, including my half brother. I began to muse that maybe I'd even passed him on the street unknowingly, or stood behind him in a convenience store. Life is crazy like that. We all seem to have these random connections, just like when my old high school girlfriend was the funeral director at my other half-brother's funeral.

I was a bit scared when I called him. I practiced my opening speech more than once, hoping to get it right, hoping to say things in a way that would not get him angry or offend him. I introduced myself by saying I was Ruth's son. That got his attention. Perhaps he already knew Ruth had some children. In either case, he was intrigued, but not incredulous. As I continued, I finally and almost passively, said, "And you and I are half-brothers."

That was the shot that did it. He was blown away and it took him a few minutes to get it back together. Those few moments were some of the longest moments in my life, but I knew my half brother had every right to them so I waited. We started talking again and he let me tell him my entire story. He listened respectfully and asked all the right questions. I kept measuring his voice and his demeanor. Yes, he was shocked, but he did not seem offended by me or my existence. All told, he seemed rather mature, serious, and well-grounded. I could find no anger or hate in his heart. I ended by saying I was planning on being in Des Moines for a few more days and that I would love to meet him. My half brother's work schedule was tight but together we managed to arrange for him to meet me at the airport on the day I was leaving, in order to see me off.

I was sitting in the common area in the airport, looking off in numerous directions, not sure where my half brother would be coming from. Finally, I saw someone approaching and he came up and introduced himself to me. His entire demeanor was open and welcoming, even before he said barely a word. One of the first things he said to me was, "I saw you from way back there, before you saw me. I looked in your direction and you weren't looking at me, but I could tell immediately that you were my brother."

I asked him why. He said with a chuckle, "Because you look more like my dad than I do!"

We talked for a while and it was quite pleasant. I couldn't help but notice that, like that first line of his, he kept saying, "My dad; my dad;" and at that time, never "Our dad." But I let it go, that would come with time I supposed.

My half brother looked a little like me, perhaps more than most other relatives I had previously met. He was a lot thinner than I and with his receding hairline, almost-white hair, white sideburns, and crow's feet around the eyes; he appeared about ten years older. Looking at him, I began to imagine myself in a few years. But he was right about Harter. The major difference between the two of us is that I did favor *our* father's looks more than he.

The talk ended well and we exchanged phone numbers. It easily could have morphed into nothingness, but my half brother was good.

He kept in touch, calling me on birthdays and holidays in order to catch up. Without making a big dramatic deal about it, he seemed to be accepting me as a relative, a brother of sorts. Over time, he seemed to become more and more in need of our relationship actually, which was nice, and I suppose I did as well.

I don't blame anyone for having their guard up when some stranger comes to the door claiming to be a long-lost family member, but with the passage of time, any initial anxieties were cleared up by virtue of my personal integrity. I asked nothing of these people, any of these people, except for contact and casual discussion. A photograph perhaps, if they were willing to spare one, or some old newspaper clipping, but outside of that it was just one human being trying to make a personal and spiritual connection with another.

About a year after my half brother and I first hooked up I got an email from someone from the 487th Bombing Group website. I had posted a picture of Harter and identified him as "my father," asking anyone who visited the site to please get in contact with me if they knew him or knew of him; querying whether anyone had flown with him the war, etc. Lo and behold, I also had a half sister, and she somehow found this reference and contacted the owner of the Bomb Group website, asking who was this guy representing himself as the son of "her" dad. A blessing really, as I had been thinking about how I could enter her life. I knew the website owner from other correspondences, so he forwarded me the email inquiry and suggested I contact this lady. I sent her an email and explained to her for the first time that she, too, had a half-brother. She and I eventually talked on the phone and I'm sure the initial discovery was a lot for her to handle. That was my entré to my half sister Ginger Hull Costanzo.

Just like with my half brother, this could have been contentious and gone south rather quickly, but again, I made my case in a forthright and sincere manner and managed to win her over. I meant no one harm; it was just that, like most adoptees, I'd been searching for my roots and was trying to find them. She understood and we soon became pen pals – emails, Facebook, texting, the works. Eventually I was even invited to the wedding of one of her daughters, which I gladly accepted. I met Ginger's husband and their family. Being married over 30 years, Ginger described Joe as her first and last love, her best friend, her Rock. This was very evident, and the benefits to the family we met appeared very clear as well. I think that helped connect Ginger and I in a way we hadn't expected. It was good, good for both of us.

Before meeting my half brother and Ginger, I had not thought of my birth father as having children other than myself. The process of finding and getting to know them expanded a window to my world that I hadn't expected, and in doing so helped me to further understand 'our' father.

CHAPTER NINE

DRIVING TO SEE MY 'REAL' DAD

"His life was gentle, and the elements so mixed in him that Nature might stand up and say to all the world, 'This was a man!'"

W Shakespeare, Julius Caesar (5.5.68)

When I dated the mother of my daughter, it was an off-and-on thing, unlike most successful courtships. Perhaps that was a sign I should have paid more attention to. At one point, I had broken up with her, thinking it simply was not going to work out between us. The Kira mess still plagued my mind, to the extent that I might have had only one or two other dates before finding myself with my daughters mom, so it would be fair to say I was still rusty and out of my element in the dating game. She had been the aggressor, so to speak, calling on me often, since we both worked for the same company. Being a typical dumb guy who wouldn't know a "signal" from a woman unless it hit him on the head, I hadn't a clue there was any subtext to her overtures whatsoever. The thing is, when men and women start meeting over and over outside of work for dinner or drinks ostensibly to talk business and then the discussion strays from business—you're dating. And after a while yes, even I realized we were dating, and I began to act more like it, reciprocating her attentions.

Wise men have said, if there are things that get on your nerves when you're dating, don't ignore them thinking they will just go away, because if you get married, they will only get worse. It's true. Nothing that happened during our marriage should have come as any surprise to me given our courtship. Same disagreements, same troubles, which is why we were, for a time, broken up.

At exactly that time, I got a call from my mom in Saint John. My adopted or 'real' dad had been diagnosed with cancer. What a time to hear such a thing. Not that there's ever a good time, but I was ticked off at my ex and had said my good-byes to her, so I had that lingering on my mind, and then this happens. I was living and working in Ottawa, without my emotional support network, especially now that I no longer had a girlfriend.

No sooner did I hang up with my mom, but Alexandra's mom called. Fate is strange sometimes. I couldn't help but blurt out what my mother had just shared with me. Big mistake. But at the time, it made all the sense in the world. I did have feelings for her - mixed and confused feelings, but feelings just the same - so why wouldn't I share my unfortunate news with her? Meanwhile, the purpose behind her call was to try to reconnect with me.

"Well, you can't be alone," she said, and she came right over. Next thing you know, we're back together. Again, wiser men than I will tell you this is never a good thing. Relationships have to stand on their own. When they occur amidst trauma, they become more related to the trauma than to anything else. I was sad and upset and I needed comfort - from anyone. I would have invited over the hockey guys who beat me up in Saint John had they been the ones to call!

Dad had prostate cancer. It was quite advanced when they found it. At first they didn't come right out and say it, but shortly after the initial diagnosis, they proclaimed it terminal. It was discovered in a very unusual way. When he finally went to a doctor, his chief complaint was that he was having back pain.

A note here about my dad. Dad was not the kind of guy who went to doctors. Unless he'd cut off a limb, he felt he could just ignore the pain or whatever and keep on working. He worked in the glass industry his whole life and I doubt there was a day he didn't have cuts all over him, some of them serious, but he just applied pressure, threw on a bandage, and kept on going. No complaints. And some of those gashes were deep and any normal man would have gone and at least gotten stitches. But not Rene Doiron.

So for my dad to think a pain was bad enough that he needed to see a doctor, he must have been in excruciating, unbearable agony. It turned out the pain in his back was due to his prostate's being so cancerous, the cancer had spread to the bones of his lower back. Unbelievable. He had to have had a hundred other painful and unpleasant symptoms along the way, but he ignored them. So, too, did he ignore regular well-visits to a doctor that would have involved a prostate examination, that unfortunate thing all us men of a certain age need to do—and believe me, seeing what my dad went through, I will never complain about or put off such a thing myself! But this was not the way I ever wanted to learn that lesson.

The bone cancer was what was causing him the most pain. His prostate was pretty much shot. It wasn't said immediately, but after a few tests and visits—not many, because the situation was painfully apparent—we were all told he didn't have long to live.

After we settled into 'round 2' as a couple, she stayed by my side during the adjustment period I went through in hearing of a parent getting cancer — and she most certainly and lovingly did— so we became closer and closer in a short period of time. She would say to me, "Mike, we're not that young anymore. What are we waiting for? I want children. You said you want children. Your dad could die any day now. Wouldn't it be great if he lived to see his grandchild?" Then there were challenges with her job status starting to arise, and she articulated that she was concerned that should she lose her job, she would need to leave the country. Getting married could take the expiring work visa concern off the table.

This is not to say this was her only interest in me. But certain realities of the situation can't be ignored and deserve mention. I know they went into her thought process at the time as she had expressed her worry quite openly.

While my instincts were still not fully aligned, I fell into a 'perhaps it'll work out' mode due to the combined pressures and situation. Couldn't help myself. She was quite upfront about the work visa business, too, and I wanted to help her out. People do that for people who are just friends. I know, because Hollywood's made about a dozen romantic comedies about it. But this was real and there was enough being stacked on the side of the ledger favoring me marrying her for me to pull the trigger and do it, and do it fast. And as I said before, Alexandra was conceived on our honeymoon. As agreed upon, no time was wasted. Her personality made certain of that, as she can be amazingly front and center when it comes to her desires.

From the time they'd told him he was terminal until the day he passed, almost two years went by. Rene was a fighter to the very end. He lived to see Alexandra, which was as I had hoped. Thus, you can see how fast things moved between her and me. We went from being broken up after a rather short courtship, to being married and having and delivering a baby in less than two years. That's fast. It also added to why it simply did not last.

Dad was still able to travel—just barely—when Alexandra was born. He and Mom came to Ottawa and we took pictures of him holding the baby at our home just after returning from the hospital. It brought a tear to my eye, knowing he hadn't long for this world. Looking back, I may not have agreed with all of it—the two of us rushing into marriage during my time of crisis—but were it not for that, my father would never have seen his grandchild, and my only precious child. It's the perfect example of life's yin and yang.

Dad with Alexandra.

When someone is declared terminal, it is unusual for them just to continue along the same basic route until finally passing in their sleep. If only. Instead, there was a predicted and predicable worsening of Dad's already dire situation. With the bone cancer spreading, he soon lost the use of his legs. This was one of the final indignities for a man like him. In this world, there are sitters and there are doers. Dad was a doer. Now he was unable to walk, even with crutches or a cane. Wheelchair bound.

His need to depend on other people must have been as painful as the actual physical pain. He needed help getting into the chair, out of the chair, doing his bathroom duties, you name it. It killed him, and deep inside, I wept for the man. It's not just about the loss of life. It's about the loss of human dignity. Some handle it better than others—the whiners and complainers of the world who crave the attention of others. But nothing could be more foreign to my father than this. I'm sure it speeded up his eventual demise. From the age of fourteen, when his own father died, Rene had been a man expected to take care of himself as well as others.

These things he complained about. I never once heard him complain about the pain or the cancer. Dad complained about the inconvenience he was being to others.

Dad was also in denial, big time. As one who did not believe in doctors, he also did not believe in their dire prognosis. Terminal? Dad used to go to coffee all the time with a fellow who's also been diagnosed as terminal. That guy was still alive, and it had been years. What do doctors know?!

I spent a lot of time coming home whenever I could in order to help. Marcel and I built ramps everywhere. Dad had to eventually be moved into the downstairs—his bedroom had always been on the second floor of the house. Now we put a bed for him in the living room. We also changed the hinges and doorknobs leading from room to room in order for Dad to be able to easily open doors without having to ask Mom for help. Whatever it took for him to be comfortable, mobile, and living with as much dignity as possible, we did. We even went up to the cottage and did the same. Dad was going to live out his last days properly, if we had anything to say about it.

As time passed, Dad was in and out of the hospital quite frequently. He didn't like it; nobody does. But when we'd get that message, it was like a special signal that something was happening, something bad, and I would usually try to hightail it back to Saint John to be at his side. I wanted to be there for Mom, and I wanted to say my good-byes if need be. Dad and I were good; our scores were settled, but still, there are things you want to say, impressions you want to leave with a person who meant so much to you. I had been spending so much time looking for my birth parents that I never wanted my real parents to think I thought any less of them. I never met Harter Hull nor would I ever. Rene Doiron raised me. He was there for me. He may not have been a flying ace, but he was my pop and he was the father made me the man I am today, not Harter.

On one of those treks in to Saint John, Dad was in bad shape, but then he rallied, as he always did, and was even allowed to come back home, so I packed up again and flew back to Ottawa, arriving back home on a Sunday night.

The next morning, a typical workweek Monday, I was driving to the office when I got a call on my cell phone from Mom. "He's back in the hospital. They brought him in again this morning. It's bad this time. Real bad. He's passing blood. They say his organs are shutting down. You'd better get home."

It was a tap on the shoulder from God. Somehow, I just knew this was it. Crestfallen, I quickly pulled a U-turn and headed back home for some clothes. I'm not a speeder, I don't roll that way, but I put my foot to the floor and gunned it.

It's a ten-hour drive from Ottawa to Saint John, which is why I usually flew. But again, I seemed to know this was it; he was about to pass away, so I didn't want to have to deal with airlines, flight schedules, early check-ins, flight delays, and all that other rot. Planes are supposed to make travel faster and easier, but it's not always the case, and this time I didn't want to have all that malarkey possibly keeping me from my father's side in his last hours. I decided to drive instead. I knew it would take a long time, but unlike a flight, I knew I was in control—or at least I had more of a sense of personal control over my schedule.

I'd only gone a few miles and wasn't even back at my house yet when a cop pulled me over for speeding. This never happens to me. He went through the typical routine, hitting me with the quippy, "You in some big hurry or something?"

Most people in this situation would have told him the truth. It could have gotten me some slack, maybe even a police escort home. But I was too inside my own head, and I'm not the kind of guy who asks for special treatment ever. "No," I replied, looking down at the floor, not even paying much attention to the officer. All he was to me was an impediment. I wasn't disrespectful or anything; just preoccupied.

The moment the officer turned his back, I threw the ticket on the floor of the car and gunned the engine again. I didn't care; I didn't give a good goddamn.

When I got home I grabbed a few clothes, among them a black suit. I knew. I just knew I'd need it. I wasn't going to go to my own father's funeral the way I went to Stephen Wilband's, wearing a polo shirt and shorts.

I got back in the car and hit the gas again, trying to make up for lost time. By the time I hit Quebec, another cop pulled me over. I was not at all surprised; I knew I'd been speeding again. He sauntered up to the side of the car exactly as had the first cop, hitting me with the same dumb question: "In some big hurry, eh?"

"No," I replied once more. I don't know what was with me, but even given this second chance, I still wouldn't share my woes with an officer of the law. Maybe it was some sort of self-loathing, that I felt I didn't deserve special treatment. Maybe it was me channeling my father, who suffered in silence through all that pain. Either way, I took the ticket, my second ticket, threw it on the floor, and raced back out onto the highway.

I got into New Brunswick and lo and behold, I get pulled over again. Three tickets, all in one day. Prior to that, I doubt I'd gotten three tickets in my entire lifetime. But here I was, in my third province, getting my third ticket, and going through the exact same routine, just as I had twice before, never mentioning why I was driving so fast. The third ticket joined the other two on the floor and I probably pulled out of that traffic stop even faster than the two before. I was only about an hour from home. I was so close I could taste Mom's home cooking. I think if a fourth cop tried to pull me over at this point, I would have floored it and given him the race of his life. I didn't care.

Thirty minutes later, thirty minutes from my destination, Marcel called me on my cellular. "Dad just passed away." It was Sept.2, 2003, he was only sixty-eight. It was all I could do not to pull over and simply cry. It was such a valiant effort, but all for naught. Dad died without me. Luckily, Marcel and my mom were at his side, which is the only thing I felt good about.

It's funny what death does to us mentally. No sooner had I pulled back onto the highway and begun what was now a much slower, less dangerously-driven ride to the hospital where my family was, my mind was set on one simple, forthright task: composing my father's eulogy. I don't know why. It was a practical thing to do and it gave me peace. Eulogies are all about how we remember people. I was remembering my dad, but in an officious way.

I believe he would have approved. I was multitasking; I was working. It's the sort of thing he would have done, although he was not known for his public speaking prowess. I assumed almost immediately that the task of delivering the primary eulogy would fall to me, so it was my job to get ready and do a good job.

It was the longest thirty minutes of my life. Planning the eulogy kept me straight, but what kept creeping into my thoughts was how I failed at my primary task, through no fault of my own. I wanted to be there before he passed. I wanted closure. Dad and I did not have any outstanding issues or debts to be paid, but still, closure is needed. Something inside me felt if I kept composing this speech, I would somehow be able to get past all that. We all knew this day was soon to come. Despite his disbelief in doctors and modern medicine, Dad was going to die soon; it was simply a matter of when. I guess that's the good part, in a way. There was no shock.

We made the funeral arrangements and things went as most funerals do. I stayed on a few days to help Mom settle Dad's affairs. My mother was quite melancholy, as would be expected. She'd spent her entire life with one man and they had a good marriage. Fortunately, she had her charity work to fall back on, but still, she was lonely at times and that saddened me. My career had taken me away from her and Saint John, which didn't help. Luckily, Marcel stayed in town and watched over her like the good brother and son he'd always been. But Marcel has his own family and they keep his hands full, so there are months when I find myself speaking to Mom more often than he does! But we all seem to make it work.

It's funny. As children, even adult children, we don't reflect that much on the dynamics of our parents' relationship with each other until one of them is gone. Then we see what happens when one half of one whole is left to stand on its own. I'd never realized, for example, that Dad was completely in charge of the family finances. Mom is smart and could have helped, but this was their way. All couples have a system and this was theirs. The problem was, it was almost like taking a kid fresh out of high school and teaching her about how a bank works, or how bills are paid. It was completely new to Mom, despite her age. I had to be very patient with her, as I learned to never assume anything in this department. I had to go with her to get her an ATM card. I had to take her to a machine and show her how to use it. The first time she tried to go solo without me, she left the card in the machine and the machine ate it and she had to get a new one.

As for the less practical things, the emotional things, I don't know if Mom has ever gotten over it. Rene was her first love and her only love. She's not dated anyone since, and at this point, I doubt she ever will. She's done as much as she can to become self-sufficient and she gets by.

Her charity work is her reason for living and she does good works, God bless her.

My ex did not attend the funeral. By this time, such a short time after Alexandra was born, we were already separated and preparing to divorce. The length of Dad's life after his terminal prognosis marked the beginning, the duration, and the end of our entire relationship, including a marriage and a child. Amazing.

Alexandra at 8.

I was already living without her, and it was tough on me. I owned a piece of investment property that I was renting out, which I planned on moving into once the renters' lease was up. I left them the home we had been living in, and while waiting for the other place to be ready, I was crashing with a friend's place – the Morin family. They were close friends, and a really great help when I needed them. That was what I came back to after the passing of my father—the life of a semi-homeless bachelor. It made it all the sadder.

Chapter Ten

The Horizon moves
as you get closer

"The years teach much which the days never knew."

~ Ralph Waldo Emerson

A FEW MONTHS AFTER THE DIVORCE, ALEXANDRA AND HER MOM moved to Raleigh, NC in the US, a place where her mother once lived prior to moving to Canada. I tried to visit Alexandra as often as I could, usually every couple months as work schedules would allow, yet I found myself getting very depressed with the complicated logistics of trying to see her regularly. I hadn't understood how difficult it was going to be living so far from my daughter, and not being able to see her regularly. After reading an article where I saw a quote by someone saying "It is only when you are old that you realize the importance of the decisions you make when you are young," I abruptly decided to quit my job and move to the US to get closer proximity and ease of access to her. It shocked a lot of people, but I was determined that I would find a way to get closer to her and participate as much as I could in her life. My ex's parents were originally from Texas, and since she was having job difficulties in Raleigh, I figured that moving to Texas might be my best bet, as there was some talk of her possibly moving there at some point in time. It was the first job change I made that had nothing really to do with my career, but it turned out to be the best decision I ever made.

As time went on and my visits to Des Moines continued—made much easier because of my relocation to the States—Ruth aged, as we all do, but when one is elderly, the changes are more noticeable. I got a few calls from the nice lady at the facility that Ruth had taken a tumble on the icy sidewalk and had to be taken to the emergency room; things like that. Old people are always falling, and I'm sure when I get older I'll fall a few times, too. I would always do what I had to do in order to help out, whether it was sending money, keeping in contact or, if something was worse than the norm, dropping everything and flying out to Des

Moines to be at her side. It was all exactly the same as I would do with my own mother, the one who raised me, and my mother knew and approved. This was an aspect of her own Christianity in action, which she lovingly passed along to me. You don't just go to Mass, you practice the teachings and you live a good and merciful life.

After Kira and then divorcing Alexandra's mother, I was so alone that it enabled me to have even more time for Ruth. Thus, Ruth may not have known it, and wasn't doing anything to actively help me during my own dark days, but she was a port in the storm for me. When I was with her, I could immerse myself in her story and her world and forget for a few days all my own heartbreak. Those days in Des Moines became a much-anticipated respite from my troubles.

Being alone has its benefits, as you have a little more time to be creative and pick up new hobbies. One such hobby I picked up, linked perhaps to an affinity of a vehicle type I drove in Canada, was the restoration of older Land Rover 4x4's. Starting with the rebuild of an older 1969 Series IIa, I picked up a couple others, a right hand drive 1961 from the UK, and also a ex-Military "Lightweight' Rover. These certainly played a good role in taking a void and filling that with something that was of great interest to me in restoring them to their old Glory. A Land Rover "Defender" hybrid soon became my favorite, and along with the masterful help of a good friend in Texas named Pat, it soon became a very unique vehicle – still my favorite, and the one that Alexandra 'tolerates' the most as well. Yet another LR restoration started in 2016, with the assistance of another Texas friend Billy Rogers, we tackled an original Defender – and did a frame and engine swap with a Range Rover classic. That project is slow but steady and will prove a favorite in the end. The progress got slowed a bit when I in parallel picked up a classic New Brunswick icon vehicle from a NY Museum swapping out floor inventory – a 1973 Bricklin SV1 ! Unknown to many around the car world as it is quite rare in numbers, but very well known to East Coasters. This 'restoration' hobby of older Land Rovers lead me to appreciate other older icons, and I picked up a 1948 Willys

Jeep from South Carolina, and shipped it up to New Brunswick for a restore project to use at my cottage during summer visits. Another skilled friend, Gerald, who lives in the area, played a great role in helping to breathe life back in towards her old glory. My appreciation in old-school antiques such as these, as well as the skills to bring them back to life grows all the time, perhaps another common DNA element reason that I was intrigued with searching for my roots.

Ever since Stephen's death and my first meeting with Ruth, I continued to visit her and keep in touch with her almost as much as I kept up with my own mother. It became a regular thing. I visited Mom in Saint John every so often; I went out to Iowa—and eventually Phoenix—every so often. It started a routine and that routine lasted years and years. It lasted through my divorce from Kira, it lasted through my relationship with Alexandra's mom, and it lasted through my days in my new life in Texas. I was the guy with two moms. It seemed a little odd at first, and I'm sure it was a little odd to other people I knew, but after a while it just became part of who I was. It probably resembled the life of a kid from a divorced family. I was splitting time between two parents—only in my case it was a birth mom and an adoptive mom. A strange feeling in some ways, in that I always felt a little guilt spending time with Ruthy, thinking about how these visits also restricted the little time I had available to spend with my adopted 'real mom' Joanie back in Canada. What made me self-justify the time however, was that Ruthy's days were ending soon, and I wanted to both provide her that special time for us – as well as to gain further insights to my "thread of life". As a gesture of inclusiveness, I would often call mom back in Canada and tell her of my latest findings, which she seemed to always appreciate.

Obviously I liked it or I wouldn't have kept up with it. It wasn't that Ruth was putting pressure on me to have a relationship with her. It just happened. We enjoyed each other's company and there were no other parties in either of our lives who gave us trouble about it. I'm sure other people in our situation might not have had things go in such a natural and lovingly smooth manner. Even had we gotten along, there's typically some grouchy person with an issue who might have given one of us grief, but in that case Ruth and I were lucky. I may have made my way through a couple marriages, but Ruth was never a sore point there. So, too our other family members. Everyone was cool.

Ruth and I kept up through my days in Canada as well as my days in Texas. She was part of my life when I finally had a child, the love of my life, Alexandra. What a blessing for that little girl; to have all those grandmas!

When Ruth and I started up, she was much older than I expected, but still in good shape and health for her age. As years went by, as with my own mother, I watched the natural deterioration that age brings.

When we first met, it was in 1993 and Ruth was sixty-four. What struck me, along with a million other things, was that she always dressed nicely. Her outfits always matched and even an average straight guy like me could tell she wore well-made attire. She was not some schlump who went out with her hair in curlers, wearing an old ratty velour track suit with food stains up and down the front. She was always maintained an appearance as a proper lady. I was impressed, pleased, and proud. I suppose a lot of this had to do with her days in fine clothing sales in New York City, as well as subsequent worldly experience, however her sisters indicated she always this way in sorts. Ruth also had caviar tastes, even if she did not always have a bountiful bank account. My mom who raised me always dressed nice, but we hadn't the financial means to match Ruth's tastes, and besides, my mother being a 'mom', her priorities were more on the kids than herself, as were my dads.

Shortly after Stephen's death, Ruth's second husband, Bill Lyman, died. That began her foray into no longer living alone, but living in various types of elderly residences. I wouldn't say these were nursing homes but, rather, they were places with smaller units, all in the same building, with nursing assistance as needed. You couldn't live there if you weren't a certain minimum age, and they had additional amenities catering to the elderly. You could come and go as you pleased and most everyone did. You also no longer had to worry about property maintenance and such. No more grass to cut, no more toilets to scrub. It was good and Ruth appreciated it.

By the time I moved to Texas, Ruth moved to a place that had more on-site nursing and so on. She'd fallen a few times and had other maladies related to general aging and it just seemed like the smartest move to make. It's funny, but with Blake and Stephen gone, I was her only natural child, and with no spouse in her life, I was it; I was her next-of-kin, the son she never knew until her later years. Yet another oddity in my thread of life journey. Sure, there were her sisters, but since they were getting up in age as well, that left either nieces and nephews or ... me.

It was an odd feeling. I looked over my mom for her small needs after dad passed, but now I had this other parent to assist as well for occasional financial and personal needs. Ruth's sister Joan also assisted much more than I in this capacity. And this person, Ruth, who had given me up once, was now in my life and I in hers - along with this growing dependency. I didn't mind. It's how I'm wired. You take care of those around you. But never did I dream I'd not only someday meet my birth mother, but that she would come to depend upon me in certain ways.

Not that Ruth was an invalid at that point, but age kept creeping up and I wanted her safe and secure. I would check in with the people who ran the places in which she resided. The way I figured it, if they knew this woman had family she kept in close touch with, they would be less apt to try to take advantage of her. Luckily, it either worked or it never was a concern in the first place. Everywhere Ruth went, her experience was rather pleasant, which made us both glad.

I would go out to Des Moines to see her a few times a year, and I would also fly her out to visit me once or twice a year. I paid my own airfare, of course, but I also paid for hers when she came to see me. It was more like how when a guy takes a girl out on a date, he usually picks up the tab. A gentleman doesn't make a big show about it, and the lady doesn't make a big deal of it, either. She was appreciative, that was for sure, but in a dignified, understated way. I wouldn't have wanted it otherwise. She in turn consistently sent Alexandra gifts for all occasions, such a custom and unique collectable dolls and the like.

Ruth started having some respiratory problems. It began with carrying those emergency inhalers, the ones that are common for asthmatics. Despite this, she was taken to the hospital more than once when the inhaler didn't work. With the passage of time, she eventually had oxygen tanks around the house with a little hose for her little nose, which further progressed to having one of those air tanks that wheeled along beside a person like a piece of luggage.

I was aware of all this as it was happening, but Ruth was rather close-mouthed and matter-of-fact about it all. She was far from a complainer or a hypochondriac. She never wanted to discuss her health. She answered questions, but only gave me as much information as was absolutely necessary. Lots of one-word yes/no answers, with as little augmentation as humanly possible. I never got the impression she was overtly hiding anything. She was simply not a whiner; was not someone who sought pity. I admired that. I try to be the same way. Maybe I got it from her; I don't know. My dad, Rene, had been the same way.

The health issues were uniform with a lot of things I noticed about Ruth. She was generally secretive without being dishonest about it. It made you wonder what else she wasn't telling you, yet again, there was nothing malicious about it. She merely kept her own counsel and didn't bother anybody.

Ironically, while not present during any of my childhood or early adult years, Ruth was with me through portions of each marriage. When I first connected with her, I was still with Kira and I paid to fly Ruth up to Ottawa to meet her. When Alexandra, my daughter was born, I flew Ruth up for that event as well, allowing her to meet my second wife. She got along with everyone and everyone got along with her. I take that for granted, but I suppose it's more unique than I give it credit for being. Ruth is pretty easy to like. She may not be the life of the party, but while party people are more memorable and charismatic, they usually have more secret enemies who dislike their flashy ways. Ruth never gave anyone who was a part of my life any reason to dislike her.

For what ever financial benefit being provided to Ruth, I never felt she took advantage of me. We'd go out for dinner, I'd pick up the check, and she would quietly thank me in a dignified manner, as if to say she could have paid for the dinner herself, but she allowed me to "be the man" and do it if it made me feel good. She didn't discuss her personal finances; most well-mannered people don't. I never talked money around her, either. Again, I'm from the "it's nobody else's business" school of thought on that matter. For most people who were raised by a parent in this situation, it would be an easy and simple conversation. For me however here, we were not quite at the stage where I could come out and discuss this openly. I had assumed however that she was comfortable.

The first time I got concrete evidence that Ruth was financially down on her luck was when I tried to reach her by phone and her line was disconnected. I panicked a little, as most children would. First I called one of her sisters, but she didn't know anything. Then I called the home where she was staying and spoke to the woman who ran the place, whose contact information I had gotten a while back and to whom I had introduced myself—as Ruth's only son, which was then the truth.

The lady got back to me and told me, hesitantly, that it seemed Ruth hadn't paid her phone bill. I gave Ruth the benefit of the doubt and assumed she simply forgot—a product of normal aging. But as time went on, it became more apparent, although Ruth did not want to admit it directly, that she was having money problems, and so I began sending her checks as needed. We didn't talk about it much. I'm sure she was embarrassed, and by not discussing it, I helped her save face.

Ruth had an almost child-like innocence about all things monetary, as if somehow, someday, "her ship would come in" and everything would be all right. But when you're an elderly woman with no job, things like that don't just happen. But it's a fallacy many people buy into—that money will simply fall into their lap one day and everything will be swell. It never happens.

Our relationship was always that of a lady and a gentleman—very old-fashioned. Old-time ladies and gentlemen didn't discuss money. Men paid and women demurely accepted. Women didn't ask for money. Gentlemen were thoughtful enough to know when they needed it and then they provided it. This was all somehow understood.

I had no problem with any of this. Were she not a dignified lady about it, I might have. If she was always on the phone whining to me about how she needed money, I may have felt taken advantage of, but Ruth was never that way. The situation was what it was and we made the best of it. She simply wasn't good with money and budgets. By this time, thank God, she'd stopped blowing money like it grew on trees, but still, since she had no pad and no savings, even her normal, regular bills were difficult to meet month-to-month.

One time I had flown over to France for a staff meeting. It was to be a very short trip, unfortunately, robbing me of the chance to make it a touristy vacation. No sooner had I arrived, I received a call from the home where Ruth was staying, telling me Ruth had been rushed to the hospital with a heart attack. They had no idea of the severity of the situation when they called. Ever hear that phrase, "Serious as a heart attack"? I took this news very seriously, and as quickly as I could, I turned right around and got myself on a plane from Paris to Des Moines. A quick phone call to Elizabeth, my executive assistant and right arm, quickly made arrangements to get me home. As I travel constantly, schedules are always challenged and frequently needing to change from original plans. Handling this dynamic as well as the maze of reporting elements needed in my role is a constant maze of confusion on a good day, but Elizabeth handles it like a machine and is somewhat of a miracle worker for me - on a daily basis.

I got to Ruth in the hospital and stuck around a few days. The longer I was there, the clearer it became this was not a massive, fatal attack at all, not that Ruth had led me or anyone to think it was. The diagnosis from start to finish was in the hands of the medical professionals, not her. After a time, they began to doubt their own initial assessment that it was a heart attack at all. This was relieving to all, but still, it was what one might refer to as a "heart episode," and that's never good no matter how you cut it, particularly at her age.

They kept her a few days, which indicated they still considered her condition serious, and then released her. I helped her get resettled into her apartment before I took off back to work. From then on we kept in even more frequent contact. It worried me I might call someday and she simply wouldn't answer. When a parent gets up in age and begins having health problems, this is what goes through your head. You stop thinking, "No answer. I'll bet she's at the grocery store," and instead think, "No answer. Oh my God, she's dead on the floor and nobody's there to help her!" It stinks, but it's a normal part of being an adult child.

It was around this time I started to talk about Ruth with her sister Joan in Phoenix. In Des Moines, Ruth really had no one. Sure, there were friends, but no one we thought she could truly count on. No family. When Bill Lyman, her second husband, passed, none of his people seemed to be on the scene, so that was no help. That would have been nice had such people been around and felt a responsibility towards her, but it was not to be.

People live where they live most times because of a lack of options. Moving to a different city or state is a major upheaval. Why do it unless there is a compelling reason? We all like our routines—the nearby church, the local grocer, the movie theater we've come to spend time at, and all our favorites places to eat. Even if we are eventually left with no family and no close friends, there are still dozens and dozens of people we have a nodding acquaintance with, people we see all the time when we are out and about. Ruth may not have gotten around as much once she grew in age, but she still had the people she knew at the home. Familiarity brings comfort, and comfort is one of the most basic things we seek in life.

Wouldn't it be better if she was, say, down near Joan, though? If she was in the same type of set-up but near a family member or two, her perspective wouldn't really change—we weren't suggesting she move in with Joan or anything—but there was that closer link in case of emergency, someone who could help make decisions if decisions had to be made.

Joan was pretty well off. Her own husband had just passed away. He had been the president of a small aviation company and having recently took ill, left Joan in a place more capable of helping older sister Ruthy. It was becoming more and more evident that Ruth and money would continue to be a problem the rest of her days. Her sister Joan provided this role from this point forward. It was wonderful to see how she took complete control of assisting her older sister.

It was decided that moving Ruth down near her sisters in Arizona would be best. Joan managed the task of helping Ruth go through all her personal things in DesMoines, to decide what would move with her. Upon her arrival in Phoenix, Ruth's health took a turn for the worse. The sunny climes of the southwest had nothing to do with it—most likely they helped rather than hurt her—nor was it anything psychological. It was just the timing. In that sense, the timing of the move was a good one. She needed more intensive care and now she was near people who cared about her.

The place we moved her into was a sort of family-based care facility, as opposed to a big nursing home. It was more intimate and she seemed to like it right away. There would be no fear of being ignored or forgotten by a huge, uncaring staff. It was almost like foster care for elderly people.

Joan and her family, and Ruth's other sisters and their extended broods, all came over to visit her as often as possible, as did I. Her sister Louise was also living in Phoenix, so that eased the load even more and made things even more fun for all the Wilband girls. Phoenix is a nice place to visit and good times were had by all.

After I took Ruth back to where she was living, I would often go back to Joan's, and Louise would still be there. The three of us would sit around chatting, usually about Ruth. It wasn't like we were plotting anything behind her back; it was simply that Ruth was obviously failing and there were things to discuss; scenarios to talk through.

The Wilband girls like their cocktails and these chat sessions would begin to resemble my times at the local watering hole with the guys. Even if the topics of discussions were, very often, dismal on the surface, with a drink in hand, we all made the best of it and still made each other smile from time to time. They were good people.

So many of the things I learned about Ruth and Harter, I learned not so much from Ruth, but from her sisters. Perhaps it was that I was Ruth's son, and mothers do not always completely open up to their own children. It is a natural instinct to sugarcoat things, to protect them. Ruth's sisters had no such compulsion with me. They let it all hang out; all the dirty laundry. There was nothing vicious about it. I think it was more of an excuse for them to relive their wild days of youth with a captivated audience, which I certainly was.

Joan belonged to a country club and she would bring Louise and I to the club—Ruth sometimes, too, when she was up to it. It is always nice to be able to share an extended family member to local friends, and it was equally enjoyable for me to meet them also. It was on some of those visits that I heard all the stories of the New York days when the girls would tear up the dance floors of the city, entrancing all sorts of interesting male characters. These were the times they'd open up and let loose with a lifetime's worth of secrets and scandals. They were entertaining me and I enjoyed it. I didn't have to pry and dig; it all came out, all of it full of laughter and reminiscence.

As time went by, Ruth became less and less mobile. Eventually, she was wheelchair-bound but still, with family around, there was often someone to wheel her around outside and to places she wanted to go and visit. We didn't mind. We'd bring her over to Joan's house for dinner and she quite enjoyed that. These were the sorts of things Des Moines could no longer offer her, wheelchair or no.

Still, with each passing month, we all saw greater and greater physical deterioration. Pretty soon, she didn't even want to get into the wheelchair and get trundled into a car or a van. We started to suspect cancer, and Ruth's condition evolved in that way. Again, I was on the road for work when I was given the news of the prognosis and again, I rerouted myself to be by someone's side.

The 'journey' of searching for my birth-parent history has also added more than only direct family members to my new expanded family circle. During the course of following various Web site interest groups, one in particular had again connected me to yet another thread of life. A posting regarding Harter prompted some additional interest beyond the one raised by my sister Ginger some years prior. I found a thread on the '487th Bomb Group' Facebook thread which referenced some discussion regarding someone looking for help identifying an Air Crew member who had signed a picture of himself to his father back in WWII. This picture was posted on the website, and was signed "Jimmie:—One of the 'Lucky Bastards', Hart".

The "Lucky Bastards Club" is a well known informal club that airmen became part of once they completed 25 missions, which in the earlier part of the war allowed them then go home. This 'club' expression later morphed to a blunt expression to symbolize the good fortune of those who could finally head home to the USA following their duty.

I almost fell off my chair to see this picture to be of my father Harter, signed to his friend Cpl. James R. Maguire, Jr., an Intelligence Officer also in the 487th BG stationed in Lavenham England at the same time as Harter. It was Cpl. Maguire's son Pete who had posted this picture looking for answers of who the soldier was that signed this to his now passed father. Pete and I immediately connected, had a long talk on the phone that weekend, and remain akin friends to this day.

From the photo collection of Cpl. James R. Maguire, Jr., Intelligence, 487th Bomb Group, Station 137, Lavenham, England circa 1945.

It is surprising how you start a search with only minimal expectations, then as you dig a little deeper, you want to find out more. Sort of like the way the horizon moves as you approach it, seeing more beauty than before. I know it sounds strange, but I had honestly, truly become like a son to Ruth. It didn't feel strange for me to act this way, nor was Ruth ever put off by my growing role in her life. It was just a natural thing we both fell into. My mom and brother in Saint John understood and had no bad feelings about it. My time with Ruth never took away time from them. I spent just as much time with them in Canada as I always had. My family was simply larger than it had been before.

CHAPTER ELEVEN

CONNECTING THE DNA

"Understanding how DNA transmits all it knows about cancer, physics, dreaming and love will keep man searching for some time."

David R. Brower

Although Ruth was now in Phoenix, I kept up with Harter's two children—my half brother and sister—who still resided in Des Moines. Life at that time became very busy for me in my work life, which impeded the progress I had hoped to make in getting to know them better unfortunately. As well, when contacting biological family as an adopted child, you often wonder if you are intruding at times by contacting them too often.

I hated to have to ask any of these people—the Wilbands as well as the Hulls—for anything, but the idea crept into my head about my having some sort of biological proof of who I was. I was a Canadian citizen. If I could prove Harter Hull was my biological father, I could also claim US citizenship. For that, I needed the cooperation of a Hull.

I took it up first with my half brother. He agreed to give saliva swabs to a lab, as did Ruth. With the DNA of a son, as well as with a mother, they were able to triangulate indicators so it was proven beyond any reasonable doubt that I was the son of Harter Hull and Ruth Wilband, one of whom was a US citizen.

I had only met my half brother that one time at the Des Moines airport, and I never yet met Ginger face to face. It was not that either of us was averse to it, but we all have lives to lead. A phone call or an email now and then seemed to be enough for all of us. My half brother is rather quiet and reserved, while Ginger is more of a powerhouse. I suppose no two siblings are exactly alike.

Like Ruth, my half brother went through a small period of personal problems, and I have been blessed to just happen to be there for him when needed, as family does.

With my half brother and Ruth's DNA data and the accompanying report, I was all set to get my American citizenship, if I cared to. When I began to move forward, though, I began to see how much harder it was then I'd first imagined. For one thing, there are no provisions on the forms about DNA proof of parental citizenship. Logic would dictate a situation such as mine would not come up every day. What they look for are the basics: birth certificates and the like. I had no official birth documents stating my identity as Harter Hull's son, only the DNA lab report.

Going the route of birthright through DNA will be a real hassle. On the other hand, I'll soon be able to apply via my green card situation, having worked in the US for nearly five years and being considered a needed skilled worker. The green card scenario is creeping up on me so fast that it just doesn't seem worth it to go through all the hassle and expense of an immigration lawyer and so on just so I can become a citizen based upon my blood lineage.

I think sometimes that situation was all just a part of my completing the circle and verifying once and for all what I had long assumed to be true once I found all these people—the Hulls and the Wilbands. Strange as it may seem, I was still a little nervous with anticipation while waiting for the results of the DNA tests, but they went off without a hitch. Ruth is my mother and Harter was my father, period, end of discussion. It was all real.

BIOSYNTHESIS

Discover the Power of DNA Testing

Post Office Box 28
Lewisville, Texas 75067-0028
800.DNA.EXAM toll free
972.420.8505 tel 972.420.0442 fax
www.800DNAEXAM.com

Final Certificate of Analysis

Case Number: 2007 P4401

Role	Name	Race	Specimen	Draw Date	Received Date
Sibling 1	Michael Rene Doiron	Caucasian	P4401SB1	6/8/2006	6/8/2006
Sibling 2	Hull	Caucasian	P4401SB2	6/12/2006	6/13/2006

Son of Harter Hull

Results:
Deoxyribo___ (DNA) isolated from the above specimens were characterized through polymerase chain reaction (PCR) at the following genetic systems:

System	Sibling 1 Allele	Sibling 1 Allele	Sibling 2 Allele	Sibling 2 Allele
B_DYS456		15		15
B_DYS389I		13		13
B_DYS390		24		24
B_DYS389II		29		29
G_DYS458		15		15
G_DYS19		14		14
G_DYS385	13	14	13	14
Y_DYS393		13		13
Y_DYS391		11		11
Y_DYS439		12		12
Y_DYS635		23		23
Y_DYS392		13		13
R_Y_GATA_H4		12		12
R_DYS437		15		15
R_DYS438		12		12
R_DYS448		19		19

Conclusion:

The data herein was obtained using the Y-STR method. Y-STRs are fou___ ___ale-specific, Y chromosome. Y-STRs are polymorphic among unrelated males and are inherited through the pa___ ___tie to no change through generations.

Son of Harter Hull

The Y-STR DNA profiles obtained from Michael Rene Doiron and ___ ... Hull match exactly. Therefore, based on results of the sixteen genetic systems listed above, it can be concluded that Michael Rene Doiron and ___ Hull are, in fact, related through paternal lineage.

I, the undersigned Director, have read the foregoing report on DNA analyses conducted on the above nam___ ___ and have verified that the results herein are true and correct. I hereby certify that these analyses have been condu___ ___ according to the standard protocols of the DNA Identity Testing laboratory, Bio-Synthesis, Inc., and are in accordance with AABB guidelines.

Son of Harter Hull

Rita Chen, Ph.D.
Associate Director
9/6/2007

Sworn and Subscribed before me thi___

6th day of September 2007

Michelle G. Albeety
Notary Public, State of Texas

Michelle G. Albeety
Notary Public
State of Texas
Qualified in Collin County
My Commission Expires
August 23, 2009

The DNA Identity Testing Center of Bio-Synthesis, Inc. is accredited by the AABB ___

DNA Tests.

I'll always relate to being a Canadian, but a part of me bristles when I'm described as *only* Canadian. My father flew thirty-eight missions for the US over Germany in WWII. I believe that makes me as American as most anyone else living in the States. I'm proud of both my heritages.

My daughter, Alexandra, has dual citizenship, which made me want it, too. I never wanted a scenario where we could ever be separated from one another by any legal means, even if for only a very short time. I love her dearly, and beyond anything legal or bureaucratic, I just want us to be the same, as family should be.

Throughout these adventurous times with Ruth, Ruth's family, and Harter's family, I, of course, kept up with my own mom. She happily and passively listened as I shared with her all the new details I'd learned about my lineage. She was curious, too, perhaps not quite as much as me, but then, who else would be?

Back up in Saint John, my mom actually met Nancy, Ruth's niece, prior to either of them knowing Ruth was my mother. Somehow I knew Saint John would provide some "small world" moments in this sojourn, and Nancy was just such a connection. My mom does so much church-related charitable work, she runs into a lot of people. Once I began filling my mom in on all the players, Nancy's name came up, and I had some pictures to show as well. "I know her!" she exclaimed excitedly. They met up again afterwards, once both of them had come to know how they were tangentially connected.

Marcel watched from the sidelines as I chased down my birth family, disinterested at first at the whole thing. But as time went on and these people became more and more a part of my regular life, I think it had an influence on him, though we never talked about it directly. I suppose he never figured it would turn out for me as it did, and once it did, it got him to thinking about his own situation.

Marcel tracked down his roots in much the same way I did. But when he felt he had discovered who his birth mother was, she told him she had no desire to meet him. Marcel is a stoic type who doesn't complain much, but I know that had to have hurt him. It hurt me just hearing about it. It made me feel guilty my situation had worked out so much better. I wish nothing but the best for my brother; I love him. There was also guilt, the same kind of guilt brothers might feel if both entered a contest and one came away with a trophy and the other did not. I had the trophy and all I could do was wish I could pass it along to him, but I simply couldn't.

Adoption is a very personal and emotional thing. People go into it for a variety of reasons and they settle it later in their minds in a variety of ways. When I came into Ruth's life, it did not rattle her cage or ruin, in her mind, what she had going for herself. Marcel's mother was different in that way. I can't recall exactly what her reasoning was or if she even bothered to say. From Marcel's point of view, there could really be no right answer, no excuse that would make him feel better deep down inside. He just wanted to connect. In the end, that's all I ever wanted from Ruth. All that came after that was just icing on the cake.

I think as Marcel attempted to connect to his mother, he passed through the life of some other relative—and aunt or an uncle, something like that—so he did have the opportunity to see and talk with someone biologically connected to him. I believe it was through that contact he was delivered the message his mother did not wish to see him. It was not for lack of trying that Marcel ran into this brick wall, the kind you sometimes cannot climb over in life. Those are the hardest things to deal with. I would never meet Harter Hull. To me, that stunk. I often think of all the things I'd like to talk to him about, but it will never happen. I came on the scene a little too late. Such is life.

I wish Marcel could have come to know his birth family as much as I did. I've never regretted a single day that I spent on this journey.

There's a funny movie, the first one Steve Martin ever made, called "The Jerk". It had this great opening line spoken by the very white, white-haired Martin: "I was born a poor black child." It always makes the audience roar because he was so sincere about it. This is nothing to do with race, just an example of deep down knowing you never quite fit in. The premise is that Martin was raised by a black family and never really gave himself up to the fact that he was, most certainly, not their biological child. Adoptees grow up like that. We can find all the love in the world within our adoptive family, but at the end of the day, when we look in the mirror, if we're being totally honest with ourselves, we can see we don't look and take on the mannerisms of the family we live with. Steve Martin with a poorer black southern family is merely taking it the extreme, but on a more subtle level, Marcel and I always felt that way living in our family. We loved them and felt a part of them. But when we looked in the mirror, what looked back, for us, were not just 'Doirons'. We didn't know *who* was looking back. Was this the world's biggest crisis? Of course not. But it stunk just the same. Now I could look in the mirror and see the Wilbands. I see the Hulls. I look at the tons of pictures I have of Harter Hull and his family and I see them in me. The best way I can describe it is … relieving. It's not enough to just know you aren't blood of the people who raised you. The complete picture is to also know whose blood you are. This in no way changes my feelings towards my 'real parents' Joan and Rene who raised me, they are truly the parents who loved and raised you always. This difference now is that the parts of me beyond the family that raised me are not so foreign and distant. Now I know, and I'm so glad. It completes me. It gives me more clarity of who one is when they truly understand the face in the mirror, and get connected to that thread of life that kids raised by their biological parents.

CHAPTER TWELVE

BIRTH MOM AND REAL MOM

"Heaven is at the feet of mothers."

Arabic proverb

As Ruth's health declined, I'd visit Phoenix more often, but I'd spend more time, too, with her sister Joan. Joan had never had children, and as age crept up on her, she openly regretted it, as people are apt to do. As the thought of Ruth dying entered more and more into the picture, along with the fact Joan's husband had already passed, she became ever more blue about "having nobody."

I said, smilingly, "To some extent, you do have a kid. You still have me around. Reality is, if it weren't for you, I wouldn't be around."

"What do you mean?" she asked.

"If you recall, Ruthie went down to Mexico with you Claire and Louise when your friend was having an abortion, and it was there she met Harter. If those events never came together, I wouldn't be here."

Her face changed as she digested it and she said, "Yeah, I guess you're right."

Her point, though, was she never had the opportunity to *raise* a child, and in that she was correct. In life, we all miss out on certain things. No one has everything. Maybe that's why there's been such debate over the meaning of the end of that great movie, "Citizen Kane". On his deathbed, this wealthy man who had everything still longed for the sled that was taken away from him when he was taken from his poor parents. Or was he longing for those parents and the poor but loving life he would have otherwise led? Either way, we always feel we're missing something. There are only so many hours in the day and so many days in a lifetime. We can't have it all, no matter what anyone says to the contrary.

I believe times I've spent with people like Joan, and discussions we've had like this, point to what I really learned throughout this entire journey. For so many adoptees, it's simply about, "I want to find my birth parents." In a way, that's no different than a dog chasing a truck. Once he catches it, what's he going to do with it? A lot of adoptees have no clue. I've spoken to some who find my connections with the Wilbands downright weird, saying, "That's something I wouldn't do. Who needs another family? You already have one!" I can understand that, I guess. But that I disagree with it is what makes us human and makes life interesting.

Ruth continued to deteriorate. Where once she enjoyed being brought to Joan's a couple times a week, it had now become a major chore, not just for her caretakers, but for Ruth herself. Consider how most people feel when they're unwell. They don't feel like doing much of anything, including getting up, getting dressed, and going out to dinner somewhere. She became more physically fragile by the day. Cancer had been definitively diagnosed and while she availed herself to certain treatments, just like it had been with my father, they eventually pronounced Ruth terminal. It was only just a matter of time.

There was certainly sadness, however death is a natural part of life, and the older one gets, the more common it becomes. Friends, relatives, they all eventually die, especially the older ones. Still, it's sad when it happens, or when it appears so clearly upon the horizon.

I tried spending as much time as possible with her, just as I had with my dad. I jumped whenever the phone rang, expecting "that call" to occur at any moment. I once flew out to Phoenix, visited Ruth in the home, then took her on one of her last trips to Joan's house for dinner. She usually made a day of it, but this time she tired incredibly after only a matter of hours and asked to be taken back.

Finally one day, the call did come. It was Joan. "She passed away in her sleep last night," she said to me. Isn't that how we all want to go? I felt incredibly sad, but relieved that her suffering had finally ended. It was 2010. Ruth was eighty-two years young.

Her sister Joan and I worked on the arrangements. Ruth had requested cremation and we honored her wishes. I flew out to Phoenix went with Joan to the cremation place, filled out all the paperwork, and completed the circle of life. We arranged a small ceremony and that was that.

We moved Ruth's things to Joan's place. By this time, there weren't many earthly possessions to speak of, but we gathered them all together and sorted through them at Joan's. Joan herself thought this might be a good time for her to make a life change by moving to Florida, Louise, too, but it wasn't something they were going to rush into, not with us still in mourning over Ruth.

I returned to Texas, melancholy. Again, I had missed being by the side of one of my parents when they died. But I was less frustrated than when it had happened with my father. If I couldn't be with him, I would have wished for him to have passed quietly and painlessly in his sleep. But he suffered to the end and my brother and mother had been at his side—everyone but me.

Ruth and I had achieved closure, perhaps even more so than with me and my father. Rene wasn't a big talker and we had no big issues to settle at the end. With Ruth, what always hung over our heads was the simple fact that she gave me up in the first place. But I know, and she knew, I was the better for it. My mom and dad wanted me so badly, and they raised me well in a home filled with love and support. No regrets. No regrets at all.

In those final days, I spoke with Ruth a lot, over the phone as she was able. I also spoke a lot with her sisters. If we couldn't all be in the same room together, we could still be there for one another. That, too, was closure. We had become a family.

Once I went back to Texas, I'm sure they wondered if I would disappear from their lives, just as I had not been a part of them for so many years prior. I had promised to stay in touch, but the world is full of broken relationships ended not by incident, but merely by neglect. But as I'd been a man of my word before, I continued to be so now. I called the sisters from time to time and we'd have wonderful talks on the telephone. I wondered if I'd ever tire of learning more about them all. There would always be another story to tell, another adventure about which I had not yet heard, and I was up for it all. They never bored me. So, too, they had become a part of my little life, wanting to know the latest on Alexandra, and my mother and brother back in Saint John, the hometown we all shared.

With Ruth's death, a chapter in my life ended, although my ties to the Wilbands and the Hulls continues. I struggled mightily to find my birth parents, as many adopted children do, and I succeeded, as many do not. For that I am grateful. I am grateful, too, for the cordial bond I was able to form with Ruth and her family, and the family of Harter Hull. That, too is rare. But with Ruth now gone and Harter having passed away many years before, and my dad Rene also passing along the way, I was now down to one parent, my sweet Mom Joanie in Saint John. Ironically the one who always is the mother to everyone, is alone herself sadly. They say it is only when you are parentless that you become a full-fledged adult. I may not agree with that, but I understand the sentiment. For those who do believe in it, I hope to remain somewhat of a child for a long time and wish my mom a long and healthy life. Luckily I had my cousins Dawn and Julie and their families in Saint John, who went to great lengths to assist in taking care of mom there. We finally got mom moved into a retirement of sorts home, and she no longer has to maintain a larger home on her own. Julie however tragically passed in 2015 due to COPD complications; creating a very sad Christmas for all that year. Julie and Dawn were older than I, and often baby-sat me and my brother growing up, and always had a very special place in my heart.

Without family like this however, life becomes a much more difficult journey for sure, so I am blessed they were so caring. My mom has been so good to me, bringing me into her life when I was just a wee breached baby trying to land on my feet, loving me and caring for me, and helping rather than hindering my journey to find my birth mother. Not many moms would do that. She's very special.

CHAPTER THIRTEEN

CONNECTING THE THREAD TO YOUR CHILDREN

"It's ok daddy, I have another grand-daddy, and you can borrow him if you like."

Alexandra Rene Doiron, at 3 yrs old
(while showing her a picture of
her deceased grandfather Rene)

I OFTEN WONDERED WHILE GROWING UP IF SOMEHOW I WOULD FIND the answers to my quest, and would those answers play a role in closing a loop for not only me, but perhaps provide a valuable 'gem of sorts' to any children I might be blessed to have. And would knowledge of my past, along with elements of my own life learning, be visible in the personality of my offspring. This may seem an obvious reality to children raised by their biological parents, but remains an unknown and invalidated data point for an adopted child. The question of nature versus nurture always seems aloof.

I like people. I like making new friends. I like traveling around. I hold onto my relationships with my oldest friends from the place where I grew up and I always will. But that never stops me from growing and exploring outside those artificial boundaries. Some of my old pals, they never left the old neighborhood. I certainly cannot criticize anyone for that, in fact admire it in many ways, but often I wondered if that would have made my life less complicated. To have deep rooted connections in a hometown, over a lifetime can create a great synergy and bond for family and friends, one I also wonder if I missed out on. We all have a right to live life in the way that pleases us, so long as we don't hurt anyone else. But I'm not scared of the unknown. The Wilbands and the Hulls were, for me, the unknown. I often wondered as an adopted child, if my "ways" were a result of my biological history, or perhaps more from my upbringing. Similarly, as I became an adult, I found myself looking at my daughter and wondering where she will get the anchors of her personality. So as child, thoughts came to me often if somehow a piece of those people who I did not know, would affect who I would become as an adult somehow.

I wonder if it all goes back to my days lying on my back in my bed, looking at my model airplanes dangling from wires above my head, imagining myself as a pilot. That came from Harter, my father, obviously, however ironically at the time I did not even know of him or his past. But he had good vision and got to do it. I didn't. Still, I had that wanderlust. Harter's took him to England and around the world. Mine has taken me places, too. Mine took me on a journey of self-discovery that I continue on to this very day. The more time I spend with the Wilband and the Hulls, the more I learn. Each email, each phone call, each visit, something new rears its head. That's the most selfish reason I do it. By now, I consider them family. Yes, biologically, they *are* family, but in some ways, that means little. Again, speaking to other adoptees, I've seen how little it can mean. My relationship with these people goes beyond biology. They are now there for me and I am there for them. But I also learn more and more about myself and it makes me take an even deeper look into my own personality and personal history. Why did I do the things I did? The model airplanes are a great example, but there are so many others. It makes me look at my daughter differently, too. All good parents study their children, but had I not found my roots, I was destined to a life where I would only be able to see Alexandra and consider how what I saw mimicked certain things about me or about her mother. That's only one layer. Ruth, Ruth's sisters, Harter, Harter's people, all the tales of the generations before them, these are the things that inhabit both me as well as Alexandra. With every generation, more material is thrown into the hopper and tamped down, like some soup in which chef after chef keeps adding ingredients.

I sometimes think I drive these people buggy with all the questions I ask, but I actually don't care as I've pursued this like rushing river of water, encountering each protruding rock or stick with quick intention to rush past it towards my goal, and they've never made me feel badly about it. I also spend a lot of time on the Internet, searching around, especially if I've recently been given some new information about a place or a company where someone lived or worked. It's interesting to me. It keeps adding to my knowledge. The "soup," so to speak, is what it is. But instead of that primordial soup just being a mystery concoction, with every discovery I learn more of what ingredients are in it. Knowledge is power. Some folks are happy just taking things as they are and accepting them without question. Me, I'm an engineer. I don't want to just ride on a train. I want to know, I need to know, how the darn thing works.

In that same spirit of self-reflection, I wonder aloud when I should begin sharing a lot of what I've come to discover with my daughter. When I first started writing this book, she was nine years old. I know when I was nine I could have cared less about all this. I didn't care about it at all during high school and college, for that matter. Still, all people—all children—are different. Boys are different than girls. I look at the situation from my male perspective. Alexandra, being a girl and being a completely different individual, may take an interest in knowing her roots at a far younger age. Girls, as they say, mature faster than boys, and perhaps my own disinterest was just another example of typical immaturity.

I think about my half brother, and I see how frustrated he was growing up in the environment he had. I get the impression he was expected to live up to a lot and he never felt he did. Me, my dad was a hard worker and a good man. That was where the bar was set for me. For me, the biggest pressure I placed on myself from that perspective was if would you become as good a man as him, and very little thoughts of ever being 'good enough' career wise. But with Harter and Harter's father, the pressure was on to be a "big shot," an entrepreneur, and a war hero, too. A war hero! It's hard to just make it as a successful, wealthy businessman. But to also fight valiantly in a war as a fighter pilot? That's a lot to load onto any young man. I don't know if I would have wanted that thrust upon me. I may have ended up living a life of self-doubt, of always feeling no matter what I did, it wasn't enough to measure up. In many ways, I had it easier.

Perhaps my half brother's situation, too, was a male thing. Do women grow up feeling as competitive and as pressured to succeed as men? God knows they're under tons of other types of pressure, but is parental competition another one of those things, or is that more on male children? I don't know, but as a parent, I worry about all these sorts of things. I always wanted to have children, and now that I have one, I obsess on it sometimes.

Ever since this journey began for me, I began studying Alexandra more and more, in ways I never did before. Who was she? Which person did she take after when she did this; when she did that? She's so much more outgoing than I was at her age, at least from my recollection. Yet I even see the folly in such opinions as that. I always saw myself as very shy when growing up. But then I talk with people I grew up with, and with my own parents, and they never describe me that way. They see Alexandra when she takes over a room, which is incredibly cute, and say, "Reminds me of you, Mike," and I think they're crazy. I always saw myself as very shy growing up. It proves that even when we look into the mirror, we don't necessarily see what others see. All my new information, gathered from my searching, has taught me more. But has it made me more accurate in my own self-perception? I don't know.

I do know this, though. I know that at the beginning, when she was first born, I watched her with far more anxiety regarding where certain traits of hers came from. That's the deep, perhaps inner insecurity of the adoptee, but more likely a more keen sensitivity and awareness of traits since an adoptee spends more time in life trying to connect dots of where they get them from. Now, I still watch her closely, but there's more of an inner peace and happiness to it. It's far more intellectual rather than emotional. Now she's a part of my "hobby," which is what my genealogy has become.

Alexandra' s mother and I have been apart since she was one year old, which is tough. At the time of this writing, Alexandra was turning 10. I had typically got to fly and see her one weekend a month, plus one or two months during each summer together - which was never enough for me. My ex never did move to Texas as I thought she would, so I was always flying from Texas or Canada to Raleigh, Wyoming, Minnesota or where ever her mom has moved, which is a hassle as anyone will tell you. Still, I do it and I'd do it even more in a heartbeat just to be there for her. I wished that I were there to tuck her in each night through those earlier years before I finally got custody when she was 10; I wish I could clean up her knees every time she fell. Instead, I was for a time that *happy weekend dad*, the one who gets to be all fun and games because he has such limited time and wants to make the best of it. Kids like their Happy Weekend Dads because they're like grandparents who dote on them and buy them everything they want. Quite often I had wished that our relationship in those earlier years would have allowed for more of the regular peak and valley experience of a fulltime parenthood role. Heck, I even hoped for days that we would have a really big argument, just like all kids and their parents do. That's the stuff that makes for realistic relationships—the good coming with the bad. I learned as much from my parents when they pulled back the reins on me as when they praised me. But Happy Weekend Dads don't get to do that as much. We also become a pawn in children's manipulation of the primary guardian parent, and I have no desire to place Alexandra's mom in such a situation, where she always has to play the bad cop and me the good cop. That's not fair to her. Before she turned 11, I was blessed to then get custody of her, and she moved in with me down in Texas. It was like a gift from heaven. I think back of the decision years back in 2005 to quit my job in Canada and move the US simply to gain better proximity to her – and realize that not having done that, I would most likely not have been able to now have her with me. All decisions we make in life, if made for the right reasons, always lead to bigger blessings.

Alexandra had a mild form of epilepsy when she was very young. Benign Rolandic Epilepsy, they call it. It took a while to get the proper diagnosis, since the symptoms are smaller than what one would expect when they hear the term *epilepsy*. She would on occasion have small seizures that were sort of like 10 second night terrors. One night when she and I shared a hotel room, I was in a light sleep when I heard this "kerplunk" in the next bed. Alexandra had fallen out of bed and onto the floor. It wasn't a big deal where she hurt herself or anything. She'd just kind of wake up groggy, then pull herself up and get back into bed. Again, not the sort of thing one would associate with a word as frightening as epilepsy.

Doctors told us she was likely to grow out of it by the time she hit her teens and I would continually pray that they were right. In the meantime, she took some medication and it seemed to work. At the time of writing this, she had been off the *meds*, as they call it, for well over two years already. So far, so good, as it appears she's kicked it earlier than predicted. That's my girl, always one step ahead.

Alexandra has a lot of Ruth in her. For as much as she can take over a room, she also has an introspective side, and when she's deep in thought, like me she also tends to look a bit pensive or unhappy with facial expression. And just like me, when confronted about it, she looks quizzically and says, "What do you mean? I'm fine."

The part where she takes over a room—and I suppose when people claim I do the same sometimes—that's got to be Harter Hull, along with a bit of myself perhaps. Everyone who knew him always said when he stepped into a room, he was immediately the biggest energy in that room. A larger than life man who loved the spotlight. Even his flight crew members recall him being that way, which is really something since when a bunch of flyboys got together there had to have been a lot of competition for the spotlight, unlike when you're the only war hero in a room full of civilians.

We had put Alexandra into a Montessori school program in her earliest school years, which involves teaching yourself as well as teaching others, which is supposed to train the mind to inquire while also teaching social skills. I used to drop her off and watch through the one-way glass outside the classroom. It was interesting to see her even more animated than when she was at home, the only child in the room. She'd be the one running around grabbing other kids and herding them over to one area or another to do things or play things. I saw extreme empathy for other as well, which truly warms my heart to see. A natural leader. It's strange watching a two or three-year-old doing that. At that point, it's sometimes a novelty just to see them noticing and interacting with one another at all.

Independence should have been her middle name. Even from her first steps, a parent's natural inclination is to step in and help. But Alexandra would become visibly upset. She didn't want anyone touching her or running her life. She knew what she wanted to do and she was just fine doing it alone, thank you very much.

By her second day of walking, she wanted to tackle some stairs. Needless to say, she was never content to rest on her laurels. If her mom or I would go over to help, even though she couldn't talk yet, she would communicate to us in some way that she wanted us to leave her alone. If she had the words, they would have been, "Back off. I've got this!"

My mom said I was similar, though maybe not as severe. The first day of school, most children cry and won't let go of Mommy's arm. Me, not only did I not cry, I didn't even want her taking me to school. I wanted to walk on my own.

Alexandra loves to laugh and make jokes. Me, she says I joke too much, but ultimately she enjoys it I feel. From what I've heard, I can see that coming from Harter. She's also very strong-willed, which propagates into being very specific on her likes, dislikes and desires. I love this independence of thought, especially at such a young age. Alexandra, despite her strength, is very, very empathetic, which I adore. It's a characteristic that I always admired in anyone who would demonstrate that.

When she was as young as two, I would show her pictures. We'd get to a picture of my father, who died not long after she was born. "Who's that?" she'd ask.

"That's your Granddad Rene." I'd say.

"He's in heaven now right?"

I'd chuckle uncomfortably, which she always intuitively picks up on. "Well, yes, he's in heaven, but he met you when you were born, got sick and died shortly after that."

She'd look at my face. From the very first moment I can remember, she could follow faces and understand people's moods, and when I said my father was dead, she could tell there was a wince in my face and voice. I loved, respected, and missed the man so much.

She blew me away that day when she read the subtle shift on my face. At less than 3 years old she said, "Daddy, that's okay," and she reached out and put her hand on my arm in order to comfort me. Then she continued, "I've got another grand-daddy and you can borrow him if you like." Wow, a dad could not feel more joy and pride than at that moment. It also made me laugh hysterically as I hugged her instantly.

> **"Daddy, that's okay,… I've got another grand-daddy and you can borrow him if you like."**

Another time we were watching TV together. It was "King Kong". When the great ape climbed the Empire State Building and planes were shooting at him, she turned to me and said, "Daddy, that's not right. They should let nature be, he didn't want to be in that city." For a three or four-year-old, that's very empathetic.

There's a silly show on now called "It Only Hurts When I Laugh", which features people falling down and getting hit in the head and other such things. Most kids love it because it is humor at its most basic. Alexandra doesn't like it. She sees people being laughed "at" or hurt and no matter what the context, it upsets her.

In Canada, we go for lobster and clams. Sometimes we don't steam them all. She'd ask, "Daddy, what are you going to do with these you left in the bucket?"

I'd say, "We're full, so we're not going to eat them."

She'd come back with, "So are we going to put them back in the water?"

Once, in a grocery store, she stopped at the lobsters in the lobster aquarium. Like most little kids, she'd sometimes get her words mixed up. She turned to me and said forlornly, "Ah Dad, look at the poor hamsters." I cracked up laughing instantly again, as did a man besides the aquarium. Simply precious moments.

When kids are really young, parents have no idea what they will be when they grow up. But it's usually pretty easy to tell what sort of people they will be, and she's going to be an asset to the world around her. We need all the nice people we can get.

I don't quite know where the strong sense of empathy in her comes from. I'd like to think a lot of it comes from me, but I've reached a point where I then try to trace my own tendencies back a generation to see where *I* got them from. Harter, I can't say I know well enough in this instance. Ruth was empathetic, but in an action-based way. If you needed something, she would go out and get it for you. She wasn't the one to put her arm around your shoulder and console you. She was more practical, almost like a stereotypical man in that sense.

As for appearances, I was blond until I was around eight years old. So, too, was Harter. He stayed more light-haired throughout his adulthood until he died at the age of fifty. My hair simply darkened. Alexandra is as blond as can be, yet her mom has jet black hair.

We have our family 'rituals' like all families tend to have. One of the most anticipated each year, is a gathering we have at the summer cottage each August during 'lobster season', where dozens of old friends gather at our summer home in Cocagne Cape for a "Rene's Retreat" get together. We have some pitch tents, others stay in nearby friends cottages, and some even crash in their SUVs. It has become the one time of the year that we take the time to catch up, enjoy company, tell tales of old, and of course enjoy some lobster. The group "crew" picture seems to grow a little each year as friends bring other friends, and also bring their own kids, as well as new neighbors join in. Alexandra at times brings friends, and often her sister Katherine comes as well. My new found sister Ginger and her husband Joe have also come and stayed as well. So in a sense, our collective 'thread of life' continues to weave a new loom each year.

true friends - you don't have be always around to be always there...

Family means a lot to me, and it breaks my heart that I don't have everyone I'd like near me all the time. I got custody of Alexandra full time in 2012, which has been a true blessing. In a perfect world, I'd also have my mom nearby, Marcel living in the same city, the Wilband sisters down the road, perhaps right across the street from the Hull kids. My childhood friends would be closer than a full day of air travel for us, and relatives could drop by the house every Sunday. In Jan of 2013, in yet another bizarre twist of fate, I like my adopted father Rene, was diagnosed with Cancer. Another little life-test to see if you're paying attention as I say; so started my own battery of treatments; lot's of CAT scans, and 'brachytherapy' for treatment, and thankfully with lots of prayers from family and friends as well. Today, I am thankfully cancer-free, and cherish more than ever the importance of close friends and family.

So Alexandra has me around thankfully for a little longer. She is very tall for her age, and Harter was taller than me, and I'm no little guy. I'm six foot even, while Harter was six foot three. Alexandra's mom is around five eight/five nine, which is tall for a woman, so I expect Alexandra can look forward to always being one of the taller girls.

On the career front, after having left Flextronics for a couple years to take on the role of of VP North America Operations at AMAZON up in Seattle, Wa., although Alexandra and I did like Seattle, we had decided that being back in Texas was best for us. So we returned to my prior company in 2014, now renamed to just "FLEX", in a role as VP Worldwide Operations for a while, then transitioned to VP of Worldwide Advanced Engineering, Quality, and Business excellence. Alexandra entered high school in grade 9, and continues to excel - and grow, at 5 foot & 8.5 inches tall at only 14 years old! She is no longer a little girl, and becoming a beautiful young lady. At this point I had full custody of her living with me for over 4 years, so I couldn't be happier about that.

All told, my journey to self-discovery as an adoptee has been as successful as any I've ever heard of. I need look no further than my own brother, Marcel, to see how often it goes the other way, where things do not work out. Speaking to or reading about other adoptees, you hear tales of them liking their adoptive mother but not their adoptive father, then meeting their birth parents and also liking one and not the other. Every possible combination can happen. For me, I don't know how much luckier one could get. I loved my dad Rene and I love my mom Joan. I loved Ruth, and everything I've heard about Harter has been pretty positive. What more could I ask for?

It's common for women who put children up for adoption to do so because they were simply unqualified to be mothers, either just at that moment in time or overall. That continues to come through when the children they gave away come to their doorstep years later. That was not the case with Ruth Wilband. I think she would have been a fine mom to me or to some other kid. It simply wasn't the right situation when I came into her body and her life, and by the time she may have reconsidered it and tried again, once she and Harter were finally together, it was probably too late for her biologically.

Still, her sisters describe Ruth as a woman best suited to being an aunt rather than a mother. Aunts can stop by from time to time and be swell around kids for a matter of hours, but once the day is done, they're happy to go home alone. Ruth, as they tell me, liked her freedom, and with kids, there is a definite lack of freedom. Agnes, the oldest Wilband sister, was acknowledged by all the other girls as the most motherly of them all. Joan never had children either, and although she's more outgoing than Ruth was, she, too, enjoyed her freedom and her "aunthood."

My mom was more like Agnes—a full-time mom. Not only that, but she was also the disciplinarian. I don't know why, but my dad frankly worked too much to have time with a lot of the traditional parenting stuff. He'd spend time with Marcel and me, but his idea of a deep man-to-man talk was to sit down and tell us a joke. I think it was because he worked so darn hard, he didn't have it in him to expend a ton of emotional energy getting into all our little day-to-day dramas like my mom was subjected to.

Marcel and I get along great and always have. He's a busy guy though, too, and like my dad, it's often hard to get him on the phone for any length of time. I respect that and I respect him. He's a good guy doing good things, whether it's his work or his family responsibilities. He doesn't waste his time being up to no good.

Marcel has three children—one of his own, and two from his wife's previous marriage. His own biological child, Joshua, and I have a special relationship. I am his god-father also. We text each other a lot and he asks me a lot about hockey and his dad —not so serious stuff—which I'm happy to help him with. I give him challenges in hockey quite often, like giving him money for each point gained during his season as an incentive. I think he really liked the added challenge as much as the incentive. With this little system in place for us, I like to have the opportunity to teach him a little about the benefits of working for a payoff at a young age, share a little more in 'family' as well. He is a special child, and Marcel does a great job with him as a dad.

It's been a long, strange journey. I guess you could say I'm a family guy at heart, but ended up with a non-traditional role in that moniker. I was the guy who right out of high school wanted a family right away. It didn't happen like that, but sometimes we have very limited control of certain things. Perhaps life has other plans for us at times, as I was actually the last guy around to *have* a family, and that certainly wasn't as I'd planned it.

Family means a lot to me, and it breaks my heart I don't have everyone with me all of the time. In a perfect world, I'd have Alexandra, I'd have my mom, I'd have Marcel living next door, and the Wilband sisters would be just down the road, perhaps right across the street from the Hull kids.

Alexandra was destined to be my only biological child, so not having her around all the time was the greatest heartbreak of my life. Until she was 10, I was with her for a long weekend usually once a month, plus had her several weeks during the summers, both in Texas as well as a few weeks in Canada at our little cottage on the bay of Cocagne. I knew that running back and forth across States to spend time with Alexandra was so very time-consuming. At the time, I couldn't imagine having to cancel any of those plans in order to be there for another child, another baby. So I decided to not have any more children. For me, this was meaningful in that what time I did have available, I could give it to her. If there is a single, solitary minute I can give to her, I want her to have it. When she was younger, like most young kids she hated talking on the phone. This however grew to be special time for her and I to talk on the phone, or Skype with video , and then later *Facetime* on the iPads. Having her call me by any method warmed my heart, and I dropped whatever I was doing to take a call with her. When she was at the age of 10, I got custody of her in Texas while her mom went into a recovery facility for a period of time. Life became instantly more fulfilling having her around fulltime. We placed her back into Montessori private school, and got her into dance classes, which excited her like a Christmas morning.

I try to keep up with the Wilbands and the Hulls to keep them in my life. Nancy is still up in Saint John and I wrote a note to myself to remind me to call her to ask if she can put me in touch with the friend of my half-brother Stephen who was with him when he tragically died. I also try to see her when I get up to my old hometown – but that never seems to work out as I would like due to family vacation scrambles when we go back North. I guess you can say the journey, for me, continues. The story may never really end. I'd like to meet everyone I have not yet met, and keep up with everyone whom I have. Will it happen? I don't know. Since finally meeting Ruth and confirming Harter as my biological father, there's been less manicness to it all. Today, I can look at it as a hobby I keep up on, like a former Olympic-caliber swimmer who used to train fanatically, but now just goes to the pool from time to time because he enjoys it. Ginger and I remain very close, either through text, email, or occasional call, we both seem to have found a post to lean on when times warrant. It is a good feeling and unexpected outcome. As well, my half brother and I stayed close via phone and email ever since. There is still much more for me to learn, and so the horizon expands as a result of my initial step to finding out more about the face in the mirror. As for the relationships I've built, I like to maintain them, just like the relationships I've maintained with the old gang from back in the neighborhood. I found that I've learned something from every rock I turned over during this journey. And similarly, everyone I meet and have spent time with in life, whether it be for 5 minutes, 5 days, 5 months, 5 years or more, I have learned something valuable to take from each exchange. This 'search' taught me the value of this.

For many adopted children there is often an ever-present curiosity about who they are beyond the upbringing they experienced. This is a very natural feeling, however many adoptees, while curious, few take on the adventure to gain the closure that stays with them for a lifetime. This has nothing to do with the quality of the upbringing provided to them by their birthparents, nor a measure of respect should they choose. While some adoptive parents may tend to try and shy away of such discussions with their adopted children, it is very important for them to understand that a desire to connect to that thread of life that non-adoptees are granted is a natural instinct – and should not be viewed as a threat to their family. The adopted child has already become part of the family the *very* day of the adoption, not because of any DNA linkage, but rather due to a mutual desire for each other, creating a bond as strong as any biologic link can offer. Support and respect from both ends of parent and child perspective is critical for such a journey to yield a healthy outcome. Done right the resulting experiences and knowledge will only be additive to both, not dilutive.

My thread of life was once just me, a single, solitary strand with no beginning and no end, only connected to people who loved me but had no other common DNA thread with me. Now my thread goes back and back for generations, and it will go on for years to come in the form of Alexandra, who will always be daddy's little girl, who I named after the street on which I grew up. It has been said in the movies, "What we do in life echoes in eternity." That is truer today than ever before for me, now that I understand my roots a little more. I can more fully appreciate my daughter's connection to them as well, and hopefully she'll never feel that disconnection I once had, when she looks in the mirror. This thread is now woven to something beyond just myself, both in my own history looking back, and also with her looking forward.

THE END ?

Alexandra at 9 yrs old, she stole my hat !